One Mykonos

Also by James Davidson

Courtesans and Fishcakes

One Mykonos

Being Ancient,
Being Islands,
Being Giants,
Being Gay

James Davidson

Thomas Dunne Books
St. Martin's Press New York

THOMAS DUNNE BOOKS.
An imprint of St. Martin's Press

First published in book form in Great Britain in 1999 by
Profile Book, Ltd.

Part of *One Mykonos* was first published in the *London Review of Books* in June 1999.

www.stmartins.com

Library of Congress Cataloging-in-Publication Data

Davidson, James N.
    One Mykonos: being ancient, being islands, being gi-
ants, being gay / James Davidson.–1st U.S. ed.
        p.cm.
    ISBN 0-312-26214-0
    1. Mykonos Island (Greece)–Description and travel.
2. Mykonos Island (Greece)– History. 3. Sex–Greece–
Mykonos Island. I.Title.

DF901.M9 D38 2000
949.5'85–dc21
                                                    00-029458

First U.S. Edition: July 2000

10 9 8 7 6 5 4 3 2 1

For Alberto,
my book, as requested,
with much love

Illustrations

i

I was dancing on an island this morning, outside
in the open air, on a mound of mythological
corpses. It was warm even before the sun came
up, which is what I had been waiting for and
when it arrived I wasn't disappointed. Dawn
reached across the island for all of fifteen minutes, groping in the dark, smoky-fingered, for the
roof of the bar of the Hard Rock Café. There she
lingered briefly, drawing a shadow, impossibly
long, out of the long, low building before finally
hitting the dance floor. At which point the flash-
ing, coloured lights were suddenly dim, the dancing stopped, and dawn disappeared in daylight.
Quantities of empty beer bottles and litter help-
fully gathered in drifts of its own accord, some
streamers, Coke cans, a plastic sachet, could no

longer be ignored. Most people had already gone home leaving the remaining dancers, about seven of us, looking like survivors, or martyrs to a cause. My friends were waiting for me, arms-folded against a wall, looking alternately at their watches and the brightening sky. We thought about getting the bus back but decided to splash out on a taxi, considering there were four of us and it was our last day.

Now it's dark again and cold and it sounds like it's pouring with rain outside and I'm wearing two shirts and two jumpers, coming from Gatwick on a train, an inch or two off midnight. A woman who's sitting opposite is asking where we've been. "Mykonos" is the most I can reply. She checks herself and looks us over. "That's the gay island, isn't it?" "Yes," I say. "It's very lively." And for no apparent reason I recall another conversation which took place ten years ago in New York, a woman talking about the children she taught, how you could spot them a mile off even at that early age: "You only had to look at them," she said of one or two boys in particular, "to see they were wearing ribbons in their hair." I can't remember seeing an image of Mykonos personified, but she would surely be wearing ribbons, except that, according to all the best sources, she wouldn't have much hair.

Modern Mykonos is a holiday resort in the Aegean, an island famous for its nightlife, a honeypot in summer where holidaymakers and homosexuals buzz tolerantly side by side, a place where a certain section of the international playset choose to moor their yachts from May to September. I've been there twice.

It's your idea of what a Greek island should look like, the one you've almost certainly heard of or seen: lots of white white cuboid churches, a labyrinthine street-structure of back passages, flowers and mounting steps, pretty windmills, brilliant sunshine, amazing beaches, the Cyclades at their Cycladicest.

Ancient Mykonos, on the other hand, sounds like a proverbial joke; like Tropical Britain, the Swiss seaboard, or Protestant Spain. It ducked out of history for the most part, keeping a very low profile indeed, "humble Mykonos" as Ovid says, a minor character in the drama of the ancient world, like Rosencrantz's girlfriend, or Guildenstern's second cousin twice removed. It is true that an Ancient Mykonian called Callidemides features in a comedy of Terence. A slave is sent to find him on the Acropolis. He is a big man, curly hair, green eyes, fat belly, a face like a corpse. The slave spends the whole day looking for him, going up to passersby asking, "Sir, are you from Mykonos?" "Sir, are you Callidemides?" but without success. The Ancient Mykonian, it turns out, is a fool's errand to keep the slave and his knowledge from spoiling the comedy's plot. He is a chimera, a wild-goose chase. He doesn't exist.

For Mykonos has never really had anything going for it apart from the beaches, no marble of Paros, ruddle of Ceos, Siphnian silver or Amorgine "silk," and ancient people weren't prepared to pay much for the pleasure of planking across its bays on water-dynamic fibreglass or swimming in seas that were particularly clear and blue or lying on expanses of properly white or golden sand or admiring a pretty view. It played its walk-on part in power games, incorporated into several empires and joining several geopolitical clubs, but it's easy to understand why it failed to make any impact on the histories. It's hard to imagine anyone fighting strenuously to take or defend it. A barren piece of granite, it was hardly a major prize. Granite is magma that solidifies more slowly, a little way underground.

If history is largely absent from Mykonos, you don't have to look far to find it elsewhere. Mykonos has an island suburb, small enough to look upon Mykonos as a mainland, fifteen or twenty minutes away by boat, more barren even than its next-door neighbour, a chip off the same piece of rock, geologically speaking. Melville called it "a barren moor." It is, nevertheless, one of Greece's most important archaeological sites, much visited by tourists and edifying cruises, honoured by several pages in all the better guides. It has a remarkable history, a very float of history, revealing history's high and low tides. It certainly had its part to play. It gets spoken to. It speaks. It's too much of a coincidence so much history and so little, side-by-side, as if the little island had somehow managed to absorb all the history in the area, Mykonos's stellar alter-ego. In fact "Star" is one of its names and some thought it fell from heaven. Now it's known as Delos.

What does Delos have that Mykonos doesn't, to have accumulated so many sculpted pieces of stone? I won't hold you in suspense, because I don't think there is much mystery about it. As soon as you encounter the island, the answer is as plain as day. Delos, as it happens, is Greek for "obvious." And here it was that Apollo, the god of light, was born, eventually, while his twin sister, Artemis, held their mother's hand.

Until then it was another kind of island, aDelos, which means the opposite of clear: vague, uncertain, obscure. So-called because it floated around aimlessly. Lucian says it was also submerged, but that's not necessary. Vagueness alone made it more or less the only place on the planet where Leto could give birth. Hera, jealous as usual, and as usual not without cause, had got wind of an affair. It was too late to stop Zeus fathering, but she tried to prevent the fathered ever leaving Leto's womb, calling on every place on earth to reject her pregnant rival, preventing the goddess of labour, which means Labour itself, from going anywhere near. This is where drifting aDelos comes into the story, fulfilling her long-awaited role. A place that wasn't strictly anywhere, it eluded Hera's curse. This is something of a set-up, admittedly, a scriptwriter's sense of a plot, but Hera, at any rate, was fooled.

It's an awful thought, an everlasting pregnancy, the babies getting bigger, kicking harder day by day—a nasty thing for one goddess to do to another. It reminds me of another piece of pedantry recorded in a strange inscription from Epidaurus, one of a series of transparent advertisements pitched at visitors to the centre of the doctor god's, Asclepius's, cult. A woman called Ithmonice had given birth immediately on leaving the sanctuary, just as the god had promised. As she had requested, it was a girl. This was her second visit and she had been carrying the child for three years. The first time she had asked the god to help her get pregnant, but she had neglected to ask him to help her give birth.

Leto landed and aDelos stopped, losing its obscurity, its alpha privative, the "un-" of "unclear."

It became instead Delos, and was "made apparent," the dramatically "revealed." Its obviousness, in this version, is not so much a state or a quality, but a moment, an event. This kind of clarity is typically Greek, turning states of being into achievements, snatched with great effort from the teeth of an opposite fate, Afters only too well-aware of what they had been Before, not being but having become, not "knowing" but "having seen," not still, but having stopped. English in its complacency loves adjectives. Greek prefers "doing" words.

I imagine it vividly, the magical synchronicity, everything happening at once, Leto landing finally – "Thank bloody god for that" – the island renamed, the arrival at the hospital, the sudden obviousness of pain. I imagine, having known some pregnant women, there was a certain desperation in that first footfall, treading on the runaway island's tail: a bit of anger, petulance even, a Rumpelstiltskinian stamp, on the verge of tears, insisting on Delos, addressing it, using its name to control it, "Delos, stay!" the stamp of an exclamation mark, "Right where you are!" the "d" of determination, the "d" of demonstrating conclusively, the "D" of QED.

This story too has wandered around a bit. I've given you only one version and the neatest pair of names. There's a lovely early poem on the subject said to be by Homer, a hymn of the sixth century Before Christ or earlier, written by a man who says he is from Chios and that he is blind. A century later, Pindar, a praise-singer if ever there was one, had a go. Then Callimachus, who reinvented poetry after Alexander making it shorter and more erudite and who catalogued the famous books in Alexandria's "Museum," two centuries after that, and countless allusions in prose. Of these my favourite is from Lucian, a satirist who could be savage, but here for a satirist curiously hesitant in tone. Iris points her rainbow bannister in Poseidon's direction and slides all the way down to his feet. "Stop that island!" she orders on landing, "Zeus commands." Says Poseidon, "Why?" "He wants it for something," says Iris, "for someone to give birth." "Aren't there enough places in the world already?" says Poseidon. "Quite so," says Rainbow, "but only this one is invisible, uncertain, aDelos, uncursed."

The early hymn, naturally, is much more numinous and respectful, "full of god," as some gay monks in Oxford kept saying to me, about someone, it may have been Cardinal Newman, they wanted canonized, when a friend of theirs had gatecrashed me into their monastery, he thought I'd find it enlightening, for biscuits and tea. What's funny, though, is how at this time the divine powers nervously, mistrustfully, haggle and deal, something God would never do. The goddess Labour is bribed to leave the side of Hera with the promise of a golden necklace fourteen feet long and Leto has to bargain with the island itself before she can give birth. "You've not got much going for you," is her opening gambit, "and a pretty lousy prospect in store. No people, no nothing, a useless tract of land. Tell you what, let's make a deal. How would you like to be the place Apollo was born?" "That's all very well," says the island, "but how will I get him to stay? He'll take one look at my desolation and leave disgusted, kicking me down with his foot. And I will be a lair for creepy-crawly sea-creatures and people won't come here and seals will be undisturbed." "I swear he won't," says Leto. "OK," says the island, "so swear!"

There's only a fragment of Pindar's version but it concerns that strange moment of revelation, the end of vagueness, the sudden stopping still. As Leto treads, four columns of adamantine reach up from the seabed to fix the island in place, pushing it firmly under her Titanic foot, reserving a place for it there. I love its realism. That's exactly what an island feels like, pushing back, resisting, when you step off onto it from a boat, as if it only stops shifting when you land on it, like particles in quantum physics or Schrödinger's magic Cat.

We must wait for Callimachus, however, before we can really go to town. His hymn is actually addressed to the island and the context is much more fraught. In the Homeric Hymn Hera keeps her counsel, the islands and other places second-guess her anger and refuse Leto out of respect. The goddess Labour isn't forbidden either, she's just kept in ignorance, distracted by some nonsense or other at Hera's side – "Before you go, one more thing ... and another thing ... I almost forgot to tell you ... Have you heard?" – the implication being that Hera doesn't want to defy her husband openly. Zeus is very much in charge. But in Callimachus, three or four centuries later, it's all battle-stations, the war of Leto's womb. Hera's helpers are posted to keep a close watch on the mistress's meandering progress. On one side Ares looks down from Mt. Pangaeum, the source of Alexander's and Philip's pre-Persian conquest gold, while Iris sits on a rock called Mimas and spies over the rest. It is interesting that it is always Iris who does the running for one side or the other in these tales of Apollo's birth. Are the poets trying to be a bit historical by painting messenger Hermes out, knowing of a famous myth in which an Apollo long after his birthdate is robbed by a Hermes one day old?

Iris is merely loyal, a dog waiting for orders by her mistress's chair, but Ares has a darker motive, knowing that once Apollo is born, he'll be second best. All powers and places feel sorry for Leto but all are too afraid. Whenever there's a hint of receiving her, Hera's henchpeople issue threats. Apollo, speaking from within the womb, tries to threaten back, "You'll be sorry when I'm born," but nobody hears or cares: a god at hand is worth two that might never emerge. That talking embryo, incidentally, is a typical example of Hellenistic tastelessness, the post-classical grotesque; and the Greeks had very intense discussions over whether and how an embryo was alive. The problem is that they called new babies "embryos" also, and didn't draw a drastic line at birth.

Leto almost persuades Peneius, a certain Thessalian river. "Couldn't you slow down a bit?" she asks. "Are you always such a torrent or is it to put me off?" Peneius relents and decelerates, turning into a lazy stream, a birthing bath. But Ares is watching closely and hits his shield with his spear, "and it rang," says Callimachus, vaguely imagining, "with a warlike noise." There's lots more growling and rumbling, as when Etna, which, says Callimachus, keeps a lid on the Giant Briareus, stirs. But Peneius has made a promise, keeps slowing, unafraid. "It's OK," says Leto finally, giving up. "I don't want your humiliation on my conscience also. I'll have to find somewhere else."

She tries other islands now and in particular Cos, but her stomach vibrates like an amplifier, that voice again, distorted in her womb. "I don't want to be born here," says the embryo, as if he has a choice. Cos is waiting for another god, a King Ptolemy, centuries hence. Alexandrian Callimachus is flattering his king and paymaster, spoiling his art with obsequiousness, being false.

Enter aDelos, the wandering isle, and Callimachus goes to town once more. Sailors, he says, would notice it on an outward voyage and miss it on the way back. The poet conveys its vagueness nicely. Its movements around the Aegean are those of an inconspicuous character, a spy perhaps, around the edge of a room, or a bush-camouflaged soldier scuttling ludicrously around. Sometimes it makes like a promontory, fixing itself to a bigger place. And it trails borrowed seaweed behind it, like a comet, which is what they call a kite in Spain. That's another nice touch, the borrowed seaweed, because a roving island, you suspect, would gather no moss of its own.

There's no bargaining in Callimachus, no caution, no special requests; just pity, humility and protestant grace. "Come on," says the island, "cross on to me. I'm not much but I'm not afraid." The poor barren island's mite. Iris reports the defection to Hera, calling Delos "the floating scum of the sea" and you realize when she says this that a floating island would indeed be on the bottom rung of the island hierarchy, a homeless vagrant, a member of the island underclass.

There are many other vague islands in Greek mythology and some of them are floating too. The nymph Calypso who keeps Odysseus away from Penelope has a luxurious one, all bosky, called Ogygia, somewhere near the Azores, way off the map, the decentred "navel of the sea." Just as floating Delos is "unclear," her name comes from the verb *calypto,* which means "I hide." There's an island called Rheneia, much closer to Delos than Mykonos even, but on the other side. It used to be called "quail-island," Ortygia, say the poets, when it was a drifter, and that was where Artemis, the elder twin, was born.

Scientists love to find truth in mythic fictions. They have discovered sound scientific reasons for the Flood of Noah in the filling of the Black Sea, for the plagues of Egypt in algal blooms, and in a peculiar combination of winds and tides, a logical explanation for the parting of the Red Sea. Some are clearly fixing things to create the reported effect. Others discover something big and assume it must have left some traces somewhere. It makes historians feel superior to see scientists being so daft, but no one doubts that islands float, like continents, according to the theory of plate tectonics that sees land as a shifting surface structure, the rearrangeable mask of Earth.

Britain has been to America and back, leaving pieces of Scotland in Canada and bits of North America along the British coast. The Appalachians, Norway and the Caledonian range were once part of the same straight line and parting was clearly traumatic. Any child with a map can see that Madagascar withdrew with its lemurs from Africa sometime before the Eocene. And the islands of the Caribbean were once Pacific, rushing in between North and South America, prevented from continuing this hokey-cokey when Panama, El Salvador etc. closed the gap. And we could see the Canaries as a single floating thing, avatars at least of a single hairline crack in the mantle pumping out hot lava mud, a single trail of magma droppings. The archipelago is an illusion produced only because the surface was floating off towards the East. Where the fault is is more like the real world, somewhere deep down. Where the islands are is the plain of images, the crust, temporary projections on the world's screen. The Canaries would have been but one Big Canary had the Earth stood still for long enough.

Big events, sure, but not fast enough. Island plates only move for geologists, indifferent to lengths of lifetime, only impressed by millions of years. We need something swifter, clearly, to make some truth of the tale. Is it possible to imagine a peculiar eruption that produces a floating bubble of rock? Or a peculiar erosion, that sand-blasts the roots of a very flat island buoyed up by some kind of bobbing stone and a fierce hurricane that blows so fiercely one day it snaps its rocky cable and sends it drifting out to sea? Or a sea-carpet of sargasso weed clogged with soil and then some plants, some ferns and grass even some trees, a natural version of the great floating fields the Aztecs invented that are still found in Mexico today? Perhaps it got stuck on a reef where Delos was lying just below the surface and perched there like a wig, a ready-made biosphere, and then the earth pushed up and the borrowed seaweed dried out and died.

It would be easy to dismiss all these floating theories as nothing more than stories, but before you go so far there's an unsolved mystery you must take account of. Delos was visited in 540 or so BCE by Pisistratus who had taken over Athens as dictator. He dug up the graves that had accumulated over the past few hundred years, whatever was in sight of the temples, spoiling the gods' putative view. They left but came again later, the Athenians, carrying spades, in 426 BCE when they were rich and powerful, post Periclean and Golden Age, at war now with Sparta and with an empire to boot. This time they dug up the whole island and removed every corpse they could find to Rheneia across the tiny strait, dumping them in what is called the Purification Trench. Henceforth there was to be no dying on Delos and no being born. Anyone who looked like doing either was hastily removed next door, which must have lent to dying the same sense of urgency a mother-to-be feels, when the pangs come at regular intervals.

In the graves they found some amazing things. Great geometric vases from Delos's archaic heyday, but they thought they were foreign objects left by an earlier foreign culture, forgetting that Greek art had once looked quite different, abstract, not at all what it had become. Their excavations were deficient. Apollo would not have been pleased. They had missed something important, something dead, something big, but not as big as it might have been: the remains of a pygmy elephant, about the size of a pony, standing only six feet tall. Little elephants have been found on other islands, Malta, Sardinia, Cyprus, Rhodes and on Sicily, *elephas falconeri,* the Sicilian dwarf. There have been theories about land bridges and the Mediterranean has emptied and filled on at least one occasion, probably more, the water pouring from the Atlantic through the straits of Gibraltar forcing animals to head for the uplands, watching their favourite pastures drown. And elephants are perfectly seaworthy over short distances. A couple were seen swimming to Sri Lanka once, but the excitement of the men who saw them arriving gave them second thoughts. They turned round and swam back.

Malta and Rhodes are of a decent size. An adventurous elephant or a stranded one might be quite happy to stay there once it had down-sized somewhat and evolved. But how could there ever have been elephants on Delos, dry and barren, not much more than one square mile? If Delos had been floating, on the other hand, all would be clear. An elephant wanders onto it once, then waits for it to settle somewhere else, somewhere green and well-watered. It grabs a passing branch and puts a temporary brake on the island, before getting off cautiously to feed. I imagine it standing alone at the prow, its ears flapping in the breeze, spying a place it would like to go next, raising her trunk for the scent of a male dripping hopefully with sperm and making a silent prayer for the future of the species. Island elephants had rounder heads and more room, therefore, for brains.

You have a short time to think such thoughts as you cross from Mykonos by boat, but when you arrive you will dismiss them, as I've said, and the reason "Why Delos?" is clear. We arrived at noon. The sea was unnaturally calm and flat. Nothing competed with the boat's unnatural wake. Only the fact that the sea stretched on for ever in all directions made you sure it wasn't a lake. We rounded the northernmost tip and squeezed between Delos and Rheneia, twin god-cots. The engine dropped a gear. In the strait an even tinier island appeared, called Hecate's, and beyond that four yachts, a huge one in the middle, old and wooden and brown, had already arrived and lay at anchor blocking the way. The yachts were quite immobile. Even the top of the mast of the big one was absolutely still. And Delos was definitely floating. When a man on the shore started pulling the rope it was clear he was coming to us.

What creates the illusion is Delos's strange form. It's like a much larger island in miniature. It has its own "river," a mere trickle of sweat, and a "mountain" down which it runs. The mountain tapers steeply down to sea level in the space of a few hundred yards, so that by the time the island hits the sea it's quite flat enough to skim on the surface, like a raft, the water washing over its ruins on one slightly listing side.

The mountain is called Cynthus, and Cynthia is a name for Artemis, as are Delia and Diana. All those fathers giving their daughters the name of a resolute virgin trying to postpone the day they would mature, none of them calling their daughter Venus or Paphia or Cytherea or Cypria in case, I suppose, she grew up to be someone's lover. It reminds us also that Delos was just as much the island of the older twin, despite those poets who tried to have her born elsewhere. In fact archaeologists strongly suspect that for years the island was hers alone, or at the very least that she was there first. And Artemis is often identified with the goddess Labour, as if it was she in one of her aspects, who kept away in order to postpone as long as possible her golden brother's birth.

Its form predestined Delos for temples and festivals and gifts. It's hard to ignore what happened, but when you look at it for the first time, it seems inevitable that such a place would appear numinous and god-filled, that those in search of something more would come here from miles around to find it. I am sure that lots of holy sites are inevitable and that if you looked at a map of the earth in year zero on the eve of the day the first person evolved, you could make a good bet on the places that would in future attract worshippers from all over the earth, peculiar random features of the planet's surface resonating predictably with the human brain, strange rocks and landed meteorites, geysers and magic lakes, certain caves and land formations, some not-too-distant islands, Bali Hais. Our festivals would be like music and the earth would be its score.

This place might not always have been celebrated. Its resonances might have been missed by the first few visitors or forgotten or ignored for a while. It might have had to spend centuries waiting, it might be waiting still, but it would, nevertheless, I think, be waiting.

I saw something similar happening in India once, at the foot of the Nilgiri "hills." The plain was full of paddy fields which harboured a nasty worm, but in one part of it was much drier land and a giant tree which, though it rose so obviously when you approached, was invisible from afar. The tree was a phenomenon in itself, its lowest branches a flat roof over your head, straight spokes radiating without a wheel to fix them, parallel with the ground for yards, supported by some muscles thickening at the trunk, its dark mountainous canopy all the more striking, of course, after the heat and light of the South Indian sun. An opening of some sort had appeared at the base and its roots were exposed as steps down to the tree's putative heart. Tridents had been stuck around, a sign that the new god had been quickly assimilated to Shiva and a piece of now-brown palm-frond marked the entrance to the site, the threshold of the sacred zone where people had to leave their shoes. Maenads came to dance here, someone told me, momentarily full of god, but we'd missed them unfortunately, they only came on the first Wednesday of the month and their last meeting had taken place only last week. On the circumference of the vast circle another shrine had appeared more recently, around some woody knobbles already well-rubbed and shiny with sacred oil, phallic only in the Indian context where phalluses are traditionally stubs. Here on the great tree's shade's edge mountains could be seen, rising impressively behind the paddy-flats and these roots seemed like an approximate image of them. This was a bad god, someone had concluded according to bad experience or some invisible rule, and so he was propitiated with bad things (or bribed to be malevolent in a more directed way) with two cigars and booze.

It's hard for Westerners even if they don't go to church not to think of cultures rich in gods like the Greeks and Romans, as somehow at an earlier stage, static and fixed with all their silly deities, waiting to be superseded by the next revelation, something more monotheistic and clean, irrational of course, as all religions are, but somehow more rational and advanced. But Christianity is a religion deep-dyed in strangeness, not one iota more reasonable than Hinduism or the religions of Aztecs or Greeks, revivifying corpses and casting out demons, necromancy, chthonic, preoccupied with death, and in India it's reasonable Buddhism that's old and obsolete, the passing phase that built its monuments first in stone then left for greener minds elsewhere, while polytheism "lingered" on and retook India and still lives and still shifts and breathes and is not an aberration.

It's because Delos seems to float that I think Pindar with his four adamantine pillars, who called Delos "unmoving" got it wrong. Perhaps he came on a stormy day when the island would seem more solid. Perhaps he never saw it. It's true the fragment begins with "Hello Delos!" but we don't have to think of him actually shouting from the boat.

Others seem much closer to the mark. Virgil, especially, who says Delos was merely anchored, chained to Mykonos and Gyaros, implying it might at some point slip away. Mykonos is an obvious choice for a fixture. It's near and its role has often been to keep things in their place, as we will see. But Gyaros is a very strange choice indeed. It's miles away up north, out on its own, an isolated island, miles from anywhere – in the Aegean, not an easy thing to be. And for that very reason it was used by the emperors as a place for undesirables, well-born troublemakers who couldn't be killed. Is Virgil being a bit political here, is he, by making Gyaros the prison of Delos, making a point?

Leto landed and gave birth. Callimachus has her loosening her belt and leaning back against a palm tree, the Homeric Hymn has her kneeling with her arms wrapped around its trunk so that Delos had a car-mechanic's view of Apollo's birth in action and rejoiced. The sweat poured off her, says Callimachus, and it looked like rain. And, as you can imagine, when her little ray of sunshine finally popped out, he turned the whole island gold. While she was in labour singing swans swam around the island, seven times, and beyond them the Cyclades, so-called because they seem like planets "circling" the island sun, an island cyclone with Delos becalmed forever in its tranquil eye.

Ares' worst fears were quickly confirmed. Apollo was immediately impressive. When he strides through Olympus only Leto stays seated at Zeus's side, says the Homeric Hymn, basking in her son's reflected glory, terribly proud. She takes his weapons off him and unstrings his bow and leads him to a seat and makes him sit down.

Temples sprang up in Apollo's honour and thousands of animals began to be sacrificed in his name. Ares, it seems, was much older and gets mentioned in Mycenaean tablets, probably, from Cnossus in Crete, but by the classical period, cults of Ares are rare. One final miracle took place at around this time. Hera stopped being angry. Something Zeus arranged.

To prove it she has a temple on Delos, one of the earliest to be built in stone, but it stands at some distance from the temples of Leto and her children and her statue faced south with her back to them. Wives could come here for empathy while their husbands were off killing cows. And they dolled her up, the dowdy wife, in a festival of her own in late August or early September.

Mortals thought they would get closer to the brilliant god if they got closer to the place of his birth, and his cult spread out from Delos like a net as first locals came, then others from much further afield. And among all the visitors were many who believed vividly that on this spot, in this Holy Month of early Spring, a god really had been born. One of the earliest fragments of European poetry is from a song the Messenians sang on arrival at Delos, many miles from their lands in the western Peloponnese. It sings of a Muse with "free sandals" which sounds ominous, as if Sparta was already threatening to still their dancing feet with chains and they would soon be helotized, a permanent race of slaves. Afters need to know where they're coming from, but Befores, also, only fully appreciate their condition, if they have a sense of what's in store. Naxos the nearest big island, much more fertile than the Mykonos rock, with woods, left more permanent monuments of its devotion to Apollo, which have lasted (but come quickly) to this day. The Naxians put their gifts in a treasure house close to the temple with Naxos's name on it, lest the god forget. They gave him a great statue, a mirror of himself and a giant of its time, and the famous lions that form a guard of honour much reproduced on postcards and soon, when the originals are finally removed from our polluted atmosphere, to be reproduced permanently in "modern" stone. But you get the impression that the locals were outclassed by their pushy cousins from the coast of Asia Minor, the rich competitive Ionians of Miletus and Ephesus, Chios, Samos and Priene, and Smyrna which finally eclipsed the rest by far, inasmuch as big is beautiful, and is known to Turks as Izmir.

The author of the Homeric Hymn flattered all of them hugely, a bit of a beggar, clearly, as well as an artiste. The men he describes are graceful, godlike and rich, their wives are well-belted and shy. He says there was boxing and dancing and singing to entertain the god, to jolly up the desert island and keep him wanting to come home, and

"daughters of Delos" who could do imperson-
ations of castanets (the text may be faulty) and of
anyone you cared to mention, so perfectly you
couldn't tell which was which. The festival was
called *panegyris* and reading the Hymn it's not
hard to see how panegyric came to mean abject
praise.

Enter Athens, not for the last time. Long considered the eldest nation of all those called Ionians, she
couldn't resist making an issue of her primacy and
getting in on the act. As it happened there had been
a civil war in Naxos. It had started, said a pupil of
Aristotle two centuries later, in an argument over
the price of fish. And the Athenian tyrant Pisistratus backed the winning side. That must have been
when he arrived with his army of gravediggers, the
purification of Delos stage one, presuming a debt of
indulgence from Naxos's new ruler and prising the
sacred island from his buddy's grip. The Athenians
might not be as rich as their eastern offshoots on
and off the greener coasts of Turkey. They brought
no lions and statues and their ships were few. But
they had a knack for something more important
than monuments, piety, and spades.

The Greeks didn't like the idea of having corpses in a living city and stationed them instead on routes out of town, which meant as you left an ancient city its ghosts would rush to meet you, saying "Think of me," "I lie here a statue where a person might have been," "I am Phrasiclea" and "Tarry a while" in stone. A sole exception was made for heroes and founders whose bones might be buried right at the city's heart. The Athenians, for instance, once thought they'd found the bones of Theseus, and put them in what they called the Theseum. For a while the Christians followed suit, sweeping dirty corpses outside the living zone in a necropolis "Corpsetown" specially built for the purpose separated from pagan tombs. But the dead insisted on snuggling up to the saints and martyrs who had been allowed like heroes in the house, knowing that martyrs whooshed straight up to heaven and hoping they would get carried along in the upwards draught, despite their heavy sins. And cities grew. The dead dug in and waited for the living to flow over them. Soon they were reconciled after a millennium and more of estrangement. Towns were founded

Delos, Apollo of the Naxians in 1445 (with inscription of Mithradates)
and in 1673 (with Mount Cynthus)

on cemeteries and people danced on graves. More recently we have become more fastidious, so we can agree with the ancients that here at least it's the Middle Ages that are strange.

Delos, however, didn't really have room for a road out of town, and until the Athenians came along, it seems, no one had really thought Apollo would mind the smell of corpses. The dead might even have tried to cling to him like Christians, keeping their corpses warm, on the off-chance, in front of the temple in the temple-reflected light. But for the Athenians Apollo had clearly become a fussy god, the god who noticed dirtiness, who provided washing facilities for murderers like Orestes who hadn't properly wiped away their stains, the god of metaphysical spit and polish, god the anti-pollutant, the god of *becoming* clean.

The Athenians came and went away again, and another tyrant arrived, Polycrates, who has tales told about him by Herodotus, from Samos, an island the Homeric Hymn calls "watered" in its list of places to which Leto didn't go. Polycrates didn't do any cleaning, but he had on board a great necklace to add to Delos's collection, a necklace as long as the one promised to the goddess Labour and he used it to make a bigger gift still, giving Delos Rheneia, its neighbour, tying it across the little strait, a dog on a lead. It is an odd gesture, chaining one island to another, but how else, short of wrapping it like Christo, do you "give" what is already there?

Polycrates went and the Persians came and the Delians left the island in a hurry. The Persians said don't be afraid and burned pounds and pounds of incense on Apollo's altars so the Delians from miles away could smell their good intentions, identifying the god of light with their own supreme Ahura-Mazda whose name later appeared on lightbulbs. In Delhi, a Muslim told me there were only two religions. There were "Book" people like us and the others, the Hindus and Persians who worship fire. The Persians worshipped fire by igniting pieces of wood stripped of the bark, covered in fat and oil. They linked fire to truth and purity. A dead animal on top would have defiled the flame inasmuch as death, like a falsehood, is dirty. This logic seems to have escaped the Greeks, except for the Orphics who offered Apollo no dead animals, but only vegetables. Among the Persians fans alone could fan the flames. Anyone who blew on them defiled them and had to be executed. After these offerings the Persians went away for a while and Delos shook for the first time.

The people of Delos watched events closely, but took their time to return. And when the Persians went for good, ten years later, there was a flotilla of Greeks chasing after them. They had attacked the mainland, not once but twice in the meantime, and burnt down Athens's temples, setting up an opposition between Apollo god of light and truth and clarity who deserved their respect and Athena god of wisdom, cleverness and deceit who didn't. But Athens pursued them bitterly for freedom, reparations and revenge, undertaking another purification, this time cleansing Greece of Persians. In the years since Pisistratus's visit, the Athenians had changed. They had thrown out the dictators and were in the process of inventing democracy; a precautionary measure to make sure dictatorship never happened again. They had found a giant silver seam locked, for some geological reason, in Attic rock and used it to arm themselves considerably with ships. And having their city laid waste by the Persians had made them very angry indeed.

Delos was made the symbolic base for military operations, and the alliance of alternately nervous, vengeful and guilty Greeks, trying to make amends for their lapse in collaborating, and not martyring themselves sufficiently for Greek freedom when it had seemed a hopeless cause, was called the Delian League. All those threats, counter-threats and punishments promised for backing the losing side must have given the island a sense of déja vu. While the Persians had been conquering left right and centre, the promises of retribution issued by the Greek resistance must have seemed as impotent as Apollo's from inside the womb, but the Persians had been defeated now and an unforgiving Athens was born.

When the Greeks captured cities from the Persians they demanded money from the citizens and "contributions for the war effort," and seized the hoarded gold. When they captured Persians they ransomed them naked, having first stripped them of their finery, which they separately sold. One famous Persian captain defied them by throwing all his treasure into the river, then removed the other source of profit by setting light to his women and children first before jumping, himself, onto the pyre. For a quarter of a century all this wealth was stored in Delos, or so we are told, but Delos doesn't have much to show for it. It didn't become, again, "gold." And Naxos's old-fashioned-looking offerings, bestowed a century before, must still have dominated the sanctuary. Symbolic centre of the greatest classical empire, Delos was in decline. It is true that when the Athenians moved the treasury to Athens in 454 BCE they left Apollo a new temple, half built, but it doesn't take thirty years to build a temple. A half built temple in fact is dangerously insulting. It must have been an afterthought.

Personally, I think the Athenians didn't trust him. His allegiance had never been clear. In Delphi Apollo had been disheartening, his oracles spreading panic, counselling no resistance at the coming of the Mede. You might forgive him once or twice but surely you would never take such a doubtful god as a squadron leader. You would certainly not prefer him to your own Athena, so reliable, so exceptionally identified with you and your cause. When the Athenians captured Eion and found the treasure chests empty and the Persian captain burnt, they compared themselves to the heroes who conquered Ilium. And models once adopted have an independent life of their own. They fix roles. If the allies were Achaeans and Xerxes Priam, that made Apollo a Persian friend; in the *Iliad* he is among the most enthusiastic of the gods who fight for Troy. Athena, on the other hand, is stalwart and military, but not in a stupid way, full of good military ideas. She, too, was honoured by the Trojans, as we will see, but she never let that affect her loyalty and having been chosen by such an effective deity, the Athenians were not about to start applying elsewhere. Making Apollo's Delos the centre of alliance must have been a concession to their allies, not the start of a new relationship; rather like putting NATO in Belgium. We are happy with Athena and we will stand by her, and you Ionians can keep Apollo, a useful god but a doubtful one, a god who swings both ways.

The *Iliad* opens with Apollo shooting plague. This was one of his specialities. When Queen Niobe boasted that she had outclassed Leto by bearing twelve children, six of either sex, Leto's children punished her by reducing the number to nothing with their darts, Artemis going for the women, Apollo for the boys. In Sophocles' lost version of the tragedy, one of Niobe's sons cries out to his boyfriend as he is dying, enough to earn it the nickname "the gay play" in antiquity, which shows how straight most tragedies were.

In the *Iliad* the Greeks earned Apollo's wrath by refusing to give his priest his daughter back. The priest was called Chryses, his daughter Chryseis, and the temple was in Chryse, that is Goldy, Golden, Gold. He had been cultivating Apollo for years, storing up a great hoard of favour, all those dead animals, all that blood on the altar. He doesn't abuse his privilege, interrupting the god with trivial news about sacrifices day and night, but the thought of his shy daugh-ter pawed and mauled by marauding campers im-pels him to make that call: "Phoebus Apollo heard his prayer and came down from Olympus, enraged. The arrows rattled on his furious shoul-der. He descended like the night. He took up a position across from the ships and shot an arrow from his bow. Terrifying was its twang." He prac-tises first on dogs and mules dropping them one by one, then he starts aiming his sharp arrows at Greeks, again, again and again. Pyres went up and day and night began to blaze. Corpses smoked. Mourners coughed.

You may not remember that, but when pyres started rising in Athens in 430 BCE, the Atheni-ans certainly did. War had been declared a year earlier with Sparta and her allies, what is known to history as "The" Peloponnesian War, though there had been at least one other. Thucydides, its historian, wandered around the plague-ridden city like a ghost, at first himself afflicted, then de-livered and, further, immune, as if by observing and writing about disease he had distanced him-self from its effects. I suspect recovery gave him the distance from the present one needs to historicize. His account of the plague is extraordinary anyway, scientific almost. He describes it in order that it might be recognized by later generations in case it reappeared, although having recognized it, what on earth would he recommend? He notes that Asclepius's doctors were the first to die through proximity to patients, revealing a precocious insight into the nature of contagion that the experts, trained to view illness as a personal imbalance, seem to have missed. Cultures can indoctrinate us with false notions, which makes historians hesitate to criticize. Thucydides is the slim but terrifying chance of truth. It may be normal in your particular environment to believe that plague is a godsend, that slaves are not human, women are giddy, Madagascar isn't going anywhere, blacks are beasts, five-year-olds want to have sex with you, your neighbour is a witch, and she and Jews and homosexuals get what they deserve, but Thucydides shows that there is always the possibility of scepticism, observation and common sense, a greater or lesser possibility, depending, but always at least a chance, a chance

Apollo and Artemis destroy Niobe's children

for anyone anywhere not to be evil or foolish, which means a chance for historians to judge the rest, although even as I am writing this I see hindsight looming mountainously in front of me, the moment of certainty passed, and wonder if there are things I don't question that will turn out to be wicked after all or, if I decide there aren't, which is definitely my inclination, that I'm being smug or Whiggish or blind. I will, however, at least insist that imagination is a very great virtue.

Thucydides observes his own immunity, noting that those who recovered didn't catch it twice or, if they did happen to catch it, didn't die. They were congratulated, recalls Thucydides, and began to imagine they could never catch anything ever again. Only they had a proper sympathy for the plague's victims. Those who hadn't yet had it were either terrified or preoccupied with doing the right thing, visiting their friends, performing the proper lamentations at whatever risk to themselves, but ignorant at the same time of what their friends were going through. Those who were dying, on the other hand, had things other than sympathy on their mind. He notes also that even though there were soon too many to burn properly and dead meat piled up in the temples and filled the streets, vultures, discovering a sudden faddishness, were nowhere to be seen. Dogs, on the other hand, who couldn't escape so easily were surrounded by temptation and occasionally succumbed. These also died, an unusual feature of this particular disease, says Thucydides, which shows that it was special. Did the great historian stand by and watch them tearing off bits of flesh without reaching for a stick? Did he see how much they swallowed and follow them around afterwards to see how long they survived? Could he have been as ghostly as that?

He dates from this time a spirit of profligacy infecting the population in the wake of the plague. Money and life seemed equally transparent. There might well be no more rainy days to hoard for and the rich died rich beside the poor, despite all their god-gifts and attendants and it was their feckless cousins many times removed who woke up unexpected heirs, where's the justice in that? The gods were indiscriminate. Good men and bad men, the generous and the mean, the pious and the scathing (a clue, perhaps, to the historian's reckless scepticism) alike were afflicted or saved, and though at first the temples were crowded with people offering prayers, they soon realized it was too late to have any effect and, defeated and exhausted, retired to their beds.

There's no mention of Apollo and his divine wrath, however, unless you read between the lines. That in many ways is what is so good and so bad about Thucydides. He is so down-to-earth that Herodotus's generous credulity, with his dreams and divine interventions, seems a world away. History here is a human affair, with no gods to pull our strings. Men are perfectly capable of making dreadful errors without any help from them. But Thucydides goes further than not believing and begins to play down belief, as if believing was just as immaterial as the illusions that were believed in, whereas, as we all know, believing can be much more real than that. This is a big mistake for a historian, but an understandable one and one endlessly repeated – to neglect, because you don't believe in God, the important fact of churches.[1]

At any rate after describing the plague concretely, Thucydides suddenly goes all vague. The Athenians went back to Delos, he says, in response to "some oracle." There were lots of these around, as always. In particular there had been a dispute over a very ancient one that someone had written down carelessly, promising either *limos* or *loimos* at the time of a Dorian War; "famine," that is, or "plague." Those who had argued for the latter suddenly felt vindicated. Of course, says Thucydides the rationalist, if there's another war with Dorians and then people starve they will simply make another textual emendation, but it's uncertain if his scepticism means he doesn't believe in gods at all or if he believes the gods have more godlike things to do than to intervene in human affairs. He knows the war that's coming will be a great one – he insists

1 That's one explanation, but there is another I would probably prefer: that Thucydides writes history in the negative, talking up what isn't talked about and saying nothing more of that which everyone knows, history that complements knowledge and is therefore necessarily incomplete.

upon it – precisely because of the earthquakes and plagues. These are not messages from angry gods; simply a demonstration that something is up. The historian had better start taking notes.

He refers to another oracle much talked-about in Athens, given to the Spartans at the start of the war, in which the god apparently had promised to do his bit for the other side and indeed the plague afflicted Athens most of all the cities and the Spartans hardly at all. Thucydides doesn't name this "god," however – that would imply it was important – but who else could it be?

Apollo had never had it so good. From this time dates his first proper temple in Rome, dedicated to Apollo Medicus, and other temples and statues were offered by cities hoping to avert the disease or, having suffered it, grudgingly grateful that he hadn't killed absolutely everyone. The temple of Apollo Helper at Bassae was one of these, says the guide Pausanias. It is one of the most beautiful temples in Greece stuck on top of a small mountain surrounded by desolate dune-like hills, like piles of sand flecked with flour. I visited it once and despite a new road with nothing to do but take people there and back down again, it was quite deserted – or so it seemed, until a guard popped out with a bread roll from behind a rock and gestured us in with his free hand, bemused that having come so far, like Columbus, we suddenly seemed so incurious. If you go there today, however, you won't have the same experience since the whole thing's now wrapped up like a present in a giant protective marquee. Though it is well preserved it's not quite as perfect as it might be. It, too, was looted by aesthetes in the last century, its sculpted friezes, the art part, carted off to the British Museum whose friends bid more than anyone else. The vandals passed through Rome at one point, and were immortalized by Ingres who sketched them.

Delphi, too, was busy. Embassies were now sent out from Athens and elsewhere to Apollo's Pythian call box to find out what had gone wrong and down the line Apollo asked in a woman's voice for a statue in Athens and then talked of Delos and her shameful decline. He could have talked of his dear Ionians and what vengeful

Athens had done to them since the Persian Wars. I am sure the Spartans, at least, thought that this was why the god was so obviously on theirs and not the Athenians' side. But Delphi chickened out of geopolitics now, a wise move, and spoke of honours and religion and religious solicitude. The priests who interpreted the priestess's divine ramblings must always have wondered how transparent they could safely be, fully aware politically, but at the same time knowing that inasmuch as they seemed political, they would seem less divinely inspired.

You can see the risk from an incident ten years later: Athens had given Delphic Apollo a Palladium from the spoils of the Persian Wars, an old-fashioned statue of Athena on a palm tree. The tree was of bronze but its berries and the Athena were gold. Hearing that Athens was about to sail for Sicily to conquer it for themselves the Delphians tried to put them off. Ravens have been pecking at that statue you gave us, they said. We thought you might like to know. The golden berries of the palm tree have fallen on the ground. We wonder what on earth it could mean.

If you are planning any big projects, cancel them. Stay at home. The Athenians simply said they were telling lies induced by Sicilian bribes. The statue wasn't broken or, if it was, they'd broken it themselves.

Ten years earlier Delphi didn't make that mistake and focused on piety. Chide Athens for neglecting Delos, but say nothing of her hubris. Look instead at all those ancient offerings from Naxos and that Hymn ascribed to Homer, souvenirs of happy days when Persians had never been heard of and Delos was where it was at, and by the same token a precise measure of how much had been lost. Thucydides, who interestingly quotes the Hymn, can't have been the only one who was amazed at the hubbub of those holidays, the singing and boxing and dancing, the well-belted ladies, the rich ships and the girl impressionists. Where had they all gone?

This time the Athenians dug up almost every dead thing and made the whole island clean. A few years later they came again, escorting all the inhabitants, even dogs, to the harbour where boats were waiting, a proper ethnic cleansing of all that potentially polluting life. They relented again, soon after, when the war started to go wrong, and let the Delians, if not their dogs, back in. They were, nevertheless, still stateless. They couldn't be born or die on Delos. They were merely residents, spending time there.

We can see the temptation of an island border, the totalizing power of coasts, that expands and squeezes the national or sacral or cultural space until it is precisely coterminous with a geographical area so the island is suddenly pure, completely free of snakes or dogs or wolves or nasty diseases like rabies, pure in a way that continents can only ever dream of. We have all felt that temptation, your body a temple, a life of carrot juice, jogging and broccoli, free of annoying friends, but few can keep it up for long.

We don't have to imagine that Apollo himself had become fussier. Unlike God God no god had ever wanted death in his or her temple and that is surely the point. There is an economy of sacred space on the island which the Athenians understood better than most. They were indeed making a gift by taking the dead away, a more spectacular gift than the Naxians' and an improvement on Polycrates' chain. It is wrong to focus on the shoddy little temples. If they had been more magnificent they would have been a distraction. They are mere chapels or sheds. Thanks to Athens, all Delos was holy now, small indeed as islands go, but the biggest temple in the world. If the Greeks had been accustomed to take their sandals off at the threshold, the sea would now have been bobbing full of them.

And having got rid of all those funless corpses, they tried to import light and life, to tempt Apollo to spend more time there and to like them a little bit more. They created a proper festival to be held every four years and went one better than boxing by putting on chariot races, managing to find space for a hippodrome on that tiny island space. You still have that sense of the whole island being a place, the place, today, since the whole island is now a site. It opens and closes at a particular hour. You could hide from the guards and have all that history, scored self-consciously in marble by Naxians, Romans, Athenians to insist on their having been there – all of that to yourself.

You buy tickets to get on the island from a little kiosk all modern and stainless steel, but entering an island is more tricky than that. To make a threshold means taking a sliver away and a turnstile means a Before and an After, and that Before means a part that isn't Delos, that isn't sacred, a part that isn't archaeologically important, that's free ... or fuzzy (or not clear). A threshold also makes coming an anti-climax, because before you go through the formalities of entering, you have already, merely by landing, clearly arrived. While you're singing "Hello Delos" a part of the island is already behind you or pushing up now under your feet. This is the first law of arriving: you only get one go. This is not so bad for us, perhaps, with our impoverished sense of process, our adjectives and stable states of being, our lack of respect for verbs, but for the Greeks a magnificent arrival, the *pompé*, which gives us our word pomp, was what people came to see. The Athenians especially were masters of coming. They were always setting off to one sacred site or another. Best of all was the one they called the "All-Athenian" when they brought

Athena a new dress, a giant piece of cloth which they carried through their city and up the Acropolis, a sacred island also, another inevitable holy site, but with a proper Entrance, the magnificent Propylaea, the Gate-in-Front. And although academics argue about it, it seems quite certain you can see images of that procession on the Parthenon's frieze, much of which of course was knocked off for London, some for Paris and a little until recently in Athens still, where Pericles put it, recklessly risking modern air.

The Messenians, then, could arrive singing of free sandals and dancing feet, and even Pisistratus could arrive and Polycrates, ready to make his *coup de don*, with the chain that might have been but wasn't a gift, and those poets, the blind man from Chios and Pindar. They could have started off on one part of the island, the more secular part the inhabitants inhabited, and get a decent runway to the sacred zone – and you need a decent runway, I think, to get a decent sacred lift – but Purification II painted them into a processional corner, pushing them off the edge. Where to line up in due order? Where to get dressed?

How to make room for arriving without taking something away? You might think it's me that's being pedantic and making problems here, but I assure you I'm being historical. These were burning issues once, contemporary concerns.

"The choirs which the cities used to send to Delos to sing for the god used to put in haphazardly and the crowd that met the ship would ask them to sing with no kind of programme or order, even as they were disembarking in a hurry and confusion, still grabbing their crowns and pulling their costumes on. But when Nicias led the Athenian pilgrimage, he disembarked at Rheneia along with the chorus and the animals for sacrifice and all the rest of the paraphernalia and then under cover of night he bridged the strait between the two islands, which isn't large, with a pontoon he'd brought with him from Athens for the purpose, made-to-measure and festooned very fittingly with gold and dyed cloth and tapestries and garlands and at dawn next day he led the procession, the choir richly costumed and singing, across the bridge and landed."

This was probably in 417 BCE and there's

something there that you have to admire, a cunning, a talent, a skill. To talk of a processional imagination, a festival intelligence wouldn't be far off the mark, the art of linear theatre direction.

The procession to Delos was one of the most extended. It started as soon as you left home. The Athenians had a sacred ship especially for it which went out to Delos with the *theoroi* ("spectators" who made the spectacle of themselves) every year. It was said to be a very old ship, the one on which Theseus sailed when he went off to be killed by the Minotaur and on which he returned having killed it. It was sent out each winter thereafter in gratitude. But after eight hundred years could it still have been sea worthy? This was a question the ancients took seriously. The ship was good to think with, and those thoughts concerned identity. Having been fixed and repaired so often could it really be said to be one and the same, this triumph of naval plastic surgery. I wonder about that myself when I see old buildings restored in the same soon-crumbling stone or when I look at pictures of myself as a baby. The only thing left of him, someone said once, is a piece of the lens in the hard centre of my eyes and if then my eyes were gouged out and burned, I might still be alive, but he would be utterly extinguished. I have to accept at least that we are vaguer than expected. We imagine ourselves as blocks of stone all solid and unchanging, but really we are a relay race and identity is a baton.

Unlike people, places have a hidden resilience. In Rome archaeologists, disaffected with digging, have walked into shops and asked if they can look in the cellar, and the owners say you don't want to go down there mate, which is exactly what they want to hear. Sometimes they find the cellars have cellars with steps leading down into the building's putative heart. And they realise they are standing on the upper storeys of a Roman house and it's the ground that has come up to meet them, rising many metres until 1000 after Christ, but only an inch for some reason thereafter. If you dug it all out taking the city back to street level, Rome wouldn't look like Rome at all but a miniature

Manhattan, dangerously teetering. But it also means, when you say "I'm going to Rome," that's exactly where you are going.

And where did they find Ilium eventually but underneath the town known to Greeks and Romans, Alexander, Caesar as Ilium, a long-lost city staring you in the face, lost only inasmuch as once Alexander's Troy had been discovered Homer's could no longer be "found."

When each year this interesting boat, which might or might not have been Theseus's, was garlanded by the priest at Phalerum, the "harbour" of Athens before Piraeus, where boats had been simply beached and Byron once had woodcock for lunch, the city took on a little of Delos's cleanliness. People still died, of course, but while the ship was away on Delos, the city refrained from helping them along and Socrates in his prison cell had to wait to be executed, an island in time where conversations could be held, the last of which was with faithful Phaedo and, while they were talking, Socrates ran his fingers through his hair. Plato recreated the scene. Perhaps he was at the edge of this intellectual circle, but he was good at imagining and very bold.

When it emerges that the boat is back, the executioner starts to mix hemlock. The holiday from killing is over. The city can get its hands dirty again. Nevertheless you will note that there will be no blood involved, too redolent of human sacrifice. Socrates asks the executioner if he is allowed to pour a little of the poison away. Potions belonged to Asclepius and he had to give the god his due libation. The executioner understands the request and doesn't laugh dismissively. He's terribly nice and civilized. But the hemlock, he says, has been calibrated precisely with none left over for sacrificial gestures.

So when the potion takes its measured effect bringing death feet first, Socrates remembers to remind his friends, even as death reaches up to his voice box, that a cockerel is owed to Asclepius, closing one account even as he opens up another. These were his last words and it reminds me of another of those inscriptions from Epidaurus. A boy falls asleep in the sanctuary. "If I cure you what will you give me?" asks Asclepius in a dream, bargaining just like Delos. "My dice," says the child childishly and the god laughs and cures him, although you wonder how the child could recount such a dream and still retain his innocence. Ancient children like modern ones were clearly performers of themselves and the adults must have understood that.

You can also detect an implication here, I think, that everyone has a right to health even if they can afford only a little, a kind of divine National Health Service or the insurance that preceded it; what my grandmother calls "the Lord George." The idea that the rich could buy more divine favour was a problem for the Greeks, upsetting their sense of fairness. There were ways around it, the idea that wealth was itself a sign of divine favour, for instance, which led the prosperous to be called "well-daemoned," although I get the impression that for most Greeks the rich were only considered blessed inasmuch as they had successfully gotten away with it; and there were also many public sacrifices paid for by the rich but given on behalf of everyone. Nicias, however, clearly thought he was getting something for himself for his money when he arrived so splendidly on Delos. If wealth meant he was favoured, he wanted to invest in that. He set up a palm tree, in bronze again, but here more resonant than in Delphi, next to the Naxians' giant statue, a thank-offering, perhaps because he too had survived the plague but was lacking Thucydides' sceptical self-confidence. He also gave the god some more land with revenues to pay for regular sacrifice and benediction and marked his gift with a stone which he left in Delos as "guardian of his gift," says Plutarch, inasmuch as it recorded forever this stipulation. Some guardian. Who owns the land now, you wonder, some farmers of olives or grapes in Attica, probably, and does any one of those farmers ever even give a thought to the piety of Nicias?

Or imagine, again, poor Phaedo taking up the baton of philosophy from a man who had run his fingers through his hair, writing dialogues, being a philosopher, even founding his own school and then discovering he had been rewritten by someone else, improved upon even, written up with such pathos, it transpires, that this version of himself had a greater chance of surviving than his own. Such is the tyranny of a talent for reproduction, that someone might do you better than you can ever do yourself, stealing away your last minutes with your dying friend by writing them up more effectively, or such is the power, perhaps, of imagination without the hindrance of having been there. It was said that Phaedo said that he had never said the words that Plato wrote for him. It was said that Plato sued Phaedo on the grounds that he acted as if he were a free man while still in fact being a slave. Would you be pleased that your name had lasted even if your features were largely distorted, or would you rather have been forgotten for good than be remembered through an impostor? It's that "largely," I think, which is the problem. Thanks to Plato at least we will never forget Phaedo's long hair, longer, thanks to Delos, than it might have been, long only as long as Socrates' life lasts, and after that cut short. And would Phaedo really have wanted all of himself to survive his own demise, even what others tell us, but Plato doesn't mention, that he had worked once in a prostitute's stall receiving clients who came for more than tea and biscuits, closing the door behind them. The *Phaedo* is sometimes called *On the Soul,* but it's not only Socrates' extinction which is in question.

So there we have Apollo: plague, prophecy, purity, gold. Does that make any sense to you? Can you see him taking shape before you? Apollo, becoming.

Greek gods, if we include all their aspects and manifestations, seem like the most miscellaneous collection, an entry in Borges' imagined Chinese Encyclopedia, not just gods of different sorts but gods of different sorts of sorts. The god in charge of weather, the one in charge of music, whose domain is water, with an aegis, who shoots arrows, who looks after cattle, is worshipped on the fifth of September, helped us in that battle then, carries torches, with white arms, frightens enemies, always seen with Aphrodite, about whom there is a story in Homer, enjoys sacrifices of unbroken cattle, of the crossroads, whose cult is celebrated at Ephesus, who comes at night, gets the first toast of the evening, invoked in the song beginning …

They all seem so polymorphous, blending into each other without discipline and even in themselves so inconsistent. A virgin goddess in charge of labour? A god of youthful brilliance and sudden death?

You can try to make sense of them. You can see gods as idiot boards, for instance, cuing primitive minds wandering around the world a few hours or so after evolution with this unaccustomed consciousness. There's a strange noise in the heavens and flashes of lightning. Suddenly you're soaking and you realize, whatever that means, it's raining. Quite inexplicable, must be Zeus. The earth shakes, must be Poseidon. The sun moving, a sun-god, the moon moving, a moon-god, an island moving, aDelos, a band of differently coloured lights bent between earth and heaven, Iris on a mission.

Alternatively you can see them as ministers with their own departments, and if they seem a bit miscellaneous sometimes it's because there has been some horse-trading. Poseidon gets seas and landslides. Zeus gets the sky and signs and mountain tops, Artemis gets hunting grounds and changes in women's bodies, Athena gets citadels and olive trees, part of war, weaving and cunning wisdom, Hades gets wealth and death, Aphrodite gets love, Dionysus gets wine, willies and drama, Demeter gets cultivation.

Or you can think of them more privately as moments of transition, when the reality of divinities you forgot about suddenly forces itself on you in the course of your day. A piece of luck, for instance, is a Hermes moment and whoever discovered the giant silver seam that built the ships that chased the Mede that created the vacuum that Athens filled so decisively, must have said at some point in his life, "What a Hermes thing!" *"What a hermaion!"* "What a god-send!" And if you feel seized by panic that's a Pan moment and you are feeling a bit Pan-ishy. Dionysus moments are more drawn out as alcohol warms your veins and you feel affected. Apollo is the morning after, remembering all the things you said and did that night, seeing clearly through the fog like an oracle, and, as the morning sun hits you, the sudden clarity of pain. Athena, then, would be that little lightbulb you still sometimes see in cartoons, and when you strike your head with your hand at the obviousness of the solution that's to let her out, her and all that wisdom. Aphrodite and Eros seem to divide amorous moments between them, a long breve and a semi-quaver. Eros is when you're sitting at a café and the girl from Ipanema passes. Aphrodite is when your lover comes home and you surprise yourself with the depth of your affection.

And then there's that special relationship with any god who will have you. That must have put pressure on gods to take on roles they were not really cut out for and the gods must have wondered, like shopkeepers anxious to keep a loyal customer's custom, if they should recommend a specialist rival or do their second best. Among those prayers offered during the plague, the ones that were so ineffectual, there must have been some to the city's great protectress. What did Athena reply? "I'll do what I can, but plague, as you know, is not really my thing. You should really be talking to Apollo. He's cornered the market in fatal diseases. Try and get him to help you. Now then, are you sure you wouldn't like some help with the olives this year, or a little cunning wisdom?"

Occasionally we get disputes between departments, as you might expect, and Athena was better placed than most to encroach as mother of bright ideas. In the fourth century, the people of Delos complained about the Athenians always muscling in on their island and the Athenians sent their best orator, silky Hyperides, to argue against them when it went to arbitration. The speech was reckoned to be one of his best. A copy must still survive somewhere in Egypt or Herculaneum, although it might already be impossible to read. We don't want to take anything away from Delos, he seems to be saying in one fragment. Everyone knows that's where Leto gave birth. But she was in Attica before that. There's a place called Belt where she started undressing. If she went to Delos instead who do you think gave her the idea?

And when a god had drawn attention to himself a little too successfully, he might find his hands temporarily full and others might fill the vacuum. At Troezen near Epidaurus it was Pan who averted the plague. He sneaked into a dream right under the nose of Asclepius with a recipe for a potion and to thank him they dedicated a temple to Pan Who Releases.

When a god takes on a function, he/she gives a particular flavour or character to the relevant events. To be cured by Apollo or Asclepius would be one thing, to be cured by Pan quite another, much more striking, releasing you from plague in a way which must be comparable with the way a panicked army goes weak at the knees, as if disease is discipline and cure a desertion.

Poseidon links horses vividly with earthquakes and Athena goddess of wisdom lent her particular colouring to Athenian war and imperialism. We can see it in Thucydides' account of the subjection of Melos, one of Delos's less proximate neighbours, the year after Nicias's visitation. Clever clogses that they are they try to *argue* Melos into submission, as if power is reason and resistance a non sequitur, although, to be sure, there are ships and weapons to help the Melians draw the right conclusion, to back up each point the Melians fail to concede.

Athena lends herself to resistance also. As goddess of the citadel she turns besieged cities into virgins, all those swords and threatening spears and bullets, so many resistible temptations.

And what of Dionysus as imperialist? He was adopted by the Ptolemies, Alexander's successors in Egypt. They soon had an empire, nostalgically reaching across the Aegean, something Egypt hadn't had for ages. Now Dionysus is an excellent god for jolly processions, but what quality does he have to help you build an empire? What does imperialism look like when it's arranged by the Minister of Fun?

In fact, I think you could go a long way with Dionysus's gung-ho ebullience: that warmth in your blood when you're getting drunk, the blood in penises rising (and if you object that there's a discrepancy here that's because the two hots are so similar), the sap that pushes out leaves in springtime and fills grapes with juice fit to bursting, and the great mass of verdant matter a creeper can produce in one season. Think of the vine reaching out with its tendrils from Alexandria, touching Delos (which flushes instantly, the famous phallus of Carystius outside his temple there, the thing visitors find funny to photograph, lifting like a dial under pressure), then covering the whole Aegean. Imagine pruning it severely then finding that within a month you're right back where you started. When you do something you really wish you hadn't and blame it on too much alcohol, when people who've been drinking arrive at your party and dominate the room, when you stand in your garden at the end of the summer and complain "the weeds are taking over," that's what it's like to be a victim of Dionysus's irrepressible imperialism.

You need a casual touch if you want to play the game of guessing a god's identity. Sometimes continuity can be discovered in only a filament. In the case of Apollo you might go for the "pl" sound, plucking a bow, plunging an arrow into someone's armpit or eye, plucking a lyre with a plectrum, the "pl" of plague and apoplexy, the plosive that hits you, light splashing off gold, or the future suddenly exploding in oracular pronouncements. The Etruscans were divinely inspired when they removed his emphatic solar centre and renamed Apollo Aplu.

As for his images, all perfect and young, it might be golden display, the nineteen-year-old who comes back newly handsome from being away, gleaming with the plasma of youthful brilliance, mother's pride, the guy in the showers, becoming clean, who flaunts a body so perfectly plastic you look away and think of mortality. Or it might just be a Before for a victim of plague, showing what you might become again.

When I did projects on Greek Mythology in Primary School, however, I wasn't that subtle, imagining, rather, the gods as superheroes. Zeus who can strike you with bolts of lightning; Apollo who can get you from miles away with his bow; Asclepius who can cure you; Demeter who can stop and start agriculture or make you feel endlessly famished; Aphrodite who can stop and start love; and any one of them who can change shape, kill you or blind you. Although I know more now about religion, this is still how a part of me tends to think of them, like the Fantastic Four, the Terrific Twelve, or the Devastating Dozen.

They're like this a lot in the *Iliad;* fighting and blasting and furious, which shows it's not a wholly inappropriate way to view them. But you know the gods are being half-hearted here since their opponents are so mortal and puny. For a real sense of gods as superheroes you have to turn to a more epic battle against enemies almost their equal, the War with the Earthborn Gigantics. Along with battles with centaurs, battles with Amazons and battles of pygmies with cranes, the Greeks loved a good gigantomachy. A battle with Giants meant a large picture with room for individual encounters, something to decorate temples and vases and countless other friezes. Unlike the other battles it also meant you could get all the gods into the picture in one go, not just hanging around on Olympus welcoming a new family member or fetching blankets and hot water for Zeus at the birth of Athena, but fighting and blasting and revealing their power, the Olympians United.

The Giants were cousins of the Olympians who rebelled at the instigation of their mother,

Delos, Phallus set up by Carystius to record Dionysian victory

Delos, Mosaic: Dionysus arrives

either because they wanted to usurp immortality or because of some offence in the deep past. The Earth was often invoked in oaths, precisely because she had a long memory. They have different names in different versions. Some are named after mountains or peaks which makes them slightly trollish. One is named after the huge cup called Kantharos. Another is called Ephialtes, the incubus who "leaps on" you at night and gives you bad dreams. Some of the names are clearly made up on each occasion.

During the battle, though accounts vary, Zeus pins them to the ground with still-rumbling thunderbolts, Dionysus uses his vine like a net to entangle a few, while from the sidelines lame Hephaestus tosses ingots of red metal or coals picked out of his furnace. Hecate the goddess of witchcraft and crossroads singes them with her attribute, two torches. Artemis's hound takes a bite out of one of them, who tries to defend himself by gouging out its eyes. Apollo shoots another with his bow.

On classical vases the Giants are armoured soldiers incongruously defeated by women-goddesses and other divine civilians. You only realize the power of these figures because the weapons they use are boulders. It's not entirely convincing. They throw them around like beach balls made of polystyrene, which is also, strangely, what they look like, fake rocks from a television programme with ambitions bigger than its budget. The most famous version of the gigantomachy, however, is very different. It decorated the Great Altar of Zeus at Hellenistic Pergamum, in Turkey, named after Troy's citadel though miles from there and well away from the coast for safety; a mighty natural fortress from which eventually to defeat the Gauls when in 278 BCE they invaded Asia Minor with their wives and families, and a good base from which to convert them into tamer Galatians and force them to settle down, but not quite remote or high enough to escape the depredations of avid antiquarians. Once Pergamum was the only city in the world with a collection to rival Alexandria's Museum, but a century ago it was itself collected and can be found in the galleries and cabinets of a building specially built for the purpose in Berlin, on an island off *Unter den Linden.*

The procession approached the back of the building that encased the altar, just as the Athenians approached the back of the Parthenon, so you had to walk halfway round the frieze before you gained an entrance. And in fact its frieze alludes to the Parthenon like an examination for art historians, alluding with the volume turned up, each incision three times deeper than its classical model and five times as close to your face, bending your ear to shout in it. The Giants are much more monstrous by now, with legs like serpents, some with bestial maws and paws, or wings that seem to provide no elevation. Giants are earthborn and earthbound, gravitating towards their mother always, their wings like those of Icarus, the sign not of flight but of plummeting. The baroque expressions of pain and suffering are cut so deep they remind you of the metaphor of "harrowing" as the Olympians and their allies sweep on, energetically pulverizing them.

You could never doubt that this was a massive effort, no suspicion of polystyrene here, an effort depicted but also an effort of depiction, since the

*Interior of shallow cup. Poseidon crushes Giant with kan-
tharos, a deep cup, on his shield*

gods are striding not only against Giants but also against the immobility of earthborn stone. And as you round its encasement, built only, you suspect, to hang the gigantomachy on, the altar itself appears at the top of a flight of steps, and the battle continues to follow you round the corner and up, tapering off as the steps rise to meet the top of the frieze, finally cutting off the decoration, and here on the steps the battle spills out into real time, hands emerge from the relief to steady themselves, knees use the same ground the sacrificers use, and their animals, to get a better footing, as if all that energy to master the Giants and move through stone has taken the figures beyond even representation, or as if the narrowing frame made by the mounting stairs produces a bottleneck of images, brimming out of bottled myth and into the spacious world, all that energy abating in the much reduced pressure of the here and now.

In the most striking section Athena grabs a young Giant by the hair, almost casually, as she's passing, a good-looking Giant who may or may not fancy himself, but has certainly been to the gym. She does exactly the same to Achilles, grabs him by the hair, in the *Iliad* to stop him killing Agamemnon, a personification of second thoughts and a vivid demonstration of the wisdom of self-discipline. The Giant's mistake, according to one version, was that he had dared to make a pass at her. He reaches over his head to grab her hand and stop her, but her snake reaches round to lick his ribs and you realize he'll have to let go. In front of her his mother, Earth, comes up from the ground interceding, suddenly evoking, incongruously, Beckett's *Happy Days.* Earth is also, as it happens, Athena's Great-Grandma, but Athena rushes on regardless, anxious to fit her head under the laurel that Victory, the only one whose wings are working, holds out for her, anxious because only when she is crowned will the viewer get the point of the scene, linking the frieze to the festival of Nikephoria, "Victory-bringing," which celebrated victory over the Galatians, connecting Virgin Athena to the integrity of the Pergamene dynasty and the Dying Giants with the Dying Gauls, and concluding both the battle and the process of interpreting it, another of those magic moments of synchronic-ity, with the answer to the question pinned safely forever in stone.

Once the Giants were subdued, there was a certain amount of tidying up to do. Only a mortal could actually kill them, so Hercules came around and despatched each one in turn with poisoned arrows while the gods held them down. Athena then did a victory dance and skinned her opponent Pallas using him as leather for her breastplate and adding his name to her own. Poseidon chipped off a piece of Cos to make a tombstone for Polybotes and a new island. There was still a bit of life left in Enceladus who was put under Aetna, Callimachus's Briareos budging up to make room, and Mimas was put under Vesuvius. He had seemed quite quite dead and the Italians happily farmed the fertile slopes of his tomb. Spartacus camped in his crater. But in the first century of our era he suddenly sprang to life again, shaking the ground, coughing up black smoke, then vomiting hot phlegm over Pompeii and Herculaneum, enveloping the inhabitants in much too mobile stone. It solidified as quickly as

Altar of Zeus from citadel of Pergamum. From l. to r.,
Giant, Athena, Earth, Nike (Victory) holding a wreath

magma, even in hot countries, is wont to. Having been liquidized for centuries Mimas was happy hard once more.

When all the gods had slaked their thirst for particular vengeance there were still a few Giants left over, dead in all their various shapes and sizes. Hercules looked around a bit to see if anyone was looking, then brushed them all under one Mykonos.

ii

I am sitting in the front row of a café on the harbour drinking a beer and eating an octopus. It's late in the afternoon and there's an air of expectation. Three ladies in slacks, about sixty- or fifty-years-old, are clutching their cameras, sitting next to me. I wonder if these are the friends of the lady who cleans the apartment for us, the ones she said she'd send there. I can't remember if we got there early to get good seats or if we had left the beach to save our skins and happened to be there by accident. It's quite possible we had been sitting there for hours, reading.

There's a fanfare and a short speech from the town square, a few hundred yards away. People clap a bit and whoop. We can see a small group leave the square and turn left towards us, preceded by two photographers walking backwards – one of them carrying a video camera, one of them whirring and clicking. It's not long before the procession hoves into view. "He's very handsome," says B. of the almost naked man on horseback. "Do you think he's a model?" Behind him six young men from the beach are carrying an image of Iris the Rainbow. It has letters stuck on to it which read "Twelve Gods Party." "Must be." All the members of the entourage have been chosen for their physique and walk behind the horse in swimming trunks. As even decent bodies do out of a context, they look a bit ridiculous. The French guy called Vincent is one of the chosen. He catches us watching and rolls his eyes heavenwards. The ladies next to us take photographs.

The man on horseback is Apollo, despite his black hair and physical overdevelopment. "What happened to the rest of them?" I can hear myself saying. "There were only seven and only one of them was a 'god,'" but B. thinks it was good fun. "Did you see that French guy we met? He looked embarrassed." We hang around a bit longer in case something else happens, then make our way back to the apartment.

The ancient Greeks had beauty competitions for men. The winners danced in the first line of choruses or led processions. Even old men might be selected or deselected, depending on their looks. It was another part of the splendour that proclaimed a city's superiority to the other Greeks, especially at the international festivals like the one at Delos: expensive gifts, the best poetry, the best singers, the most gold, the finest costumes, perfect dancers, and a wealth of handsome faces drawn from the city's gene-pool. B. is reading his beloved Beryl Bainbridge on the patio. I interrupt him to impart this interesting information. "My God!" he says. "You're like an open book."

Next day, the woman who cleans wants to know what the procession was like. I say I was disappointed. It was a man on a horse from an agency and six boys from the beach with a flag. She's also disappointed. She's from Derbyshire and introduced herself as strong in th' arm, thick in th' head which I had to explain to B. She's lived here for ages, and has a son who's half Greek, somewhere at university. Our description of the procession provokes an observation. "The Greeks," she says, "don't know how to have a good time. No really, they are very boring." I think back to a few Greeks I have known and see sometimes what she means, but one of them had to be the most beautiful (no really) man I ever met, and nice and kind, the kind of man who would have been Nicias's first choice to lead the chorus, except that he was Cefalonia's achievement rather than Athens's. He hated the Oxford climate and always said Japan with a stress on the first syllable instead of saying Japan.

We wonder which beach we are going to go to today. For the first few days we were somewhat constrained by bus timetables. But B. wouldn't put up with that and said we had to get motorbikes. I managed to beat him down to a moped after a whole day pointing out people with broken arms, raising the terrifying prospect of anything happening to me. Among beaches, there turn out to be only three choices. Superparadise is the most extraordinary. A bay slung between two promontories, the sea is green like a swimming pool, which is a compliment for a stretch of open water, equivalent to saying a landscape is picturesque, or, as B. says confusingly, "pinturesque." The most peculiar thing about the beach is the feeling it has of an enormous outside room. More remote and spacious is Elea. On the other side of the island is Ayios Sostes, which I translate, hopefully, as "San Salvador." You can find yourself almost alone here if you come just a week after high season. Superparadise on the other hand is always packed full with people and from about four o' clock in the afternoon music beats out like a disco. You have to be in seal-colony mood to have the remotest chance of enjoying it, but it is, as I said, quite spectacular and sometimes being a seal on a beach with music in the background is exactly what you feel like. Elea, on the other hand, is always a viable option, unless the wind is blowing. There are umbrellas for shade and a great beach café, which in Spain they call *chiringuito*. There are several other beaches, of course, but gay people don't go there much and we have disdained them.

The route to Superparadise runs past the runway which fits on the island as awkwardly as Delos's Hippodrome. A little off the end of it you come to a turning and have to choose between right and left. Left will take you to the straight side of the beach and right to the gay. It used to be all gay, apparently, but by now the straight people have taken over about four-fifths of it, although there is a big overlapping area where there is some integration. Some gay people who have been coming here for years are disconsolate about this development and fear for the future. The road alternates mere track with pot-holed tarmac. Eventually you see the sea, then the bay then the beach and realize you are on one edge of a shallowly pouring valley, a strange valley littered with giant boulders which do indeed look like painted polystyrene. There must be some connection between these boulders and the story about the buried Giants and you do wonder, if they weren't thrown, how on earth they got here. Only the highest parts of Greece experienced the ice age, so glaciers are out of the question. I think again about how the Giants were born from

Earth and try to recall any references to them hatching.

You know you've reached your destination when the road falls away, precipitously slipping down the valley's parabolic scoop. The road looks dangerously shiny and rubbed smooth despite the grooves scored into its surface. Some park up here where we are now hesitating, finding the inclination far too risky, but there are plenty of bikes and mopeds in the car park below to prove that many have made it. You switch off the engine, such as it is, and apply the brakes just enough to prevent reckless acceleration, but not so much that you begin to slide. You wonder if you should have hired something more powerful, knowing what you've got will never get you back up again.

If you did lose control, a cocktail bar is waiting at the bottom to catch you. Exactly like the ones you see in brochures of the Caribbean, round and thatched for shade, it looks out over the beach below. Some of the tables are arranged around the little salt-water swimming pool, which is constructed right on the edge of the high rock so only the blue of the bay is visible beyond it and the pool's perimeter looks like a thin stone line, an unnecessary breakwater. Sometimes people come to take photographs from here and then go away again. From the bar a series of stone steps lead down onto a couple more terraces and then to the beach. If you get here before about ten it will be empty apart from a flight attendant or two quickly stripping off his uniform and fitting in a swim while the cleaners clean the aeroplane, or some old hippy doing exercises while the staff of the cocktail bar comb the beach with sawn-off plastic bottles which they fill with cigarette stubs. From twelve onwards, however, the beach is crowded. You take advantage of the view from the last few steps to spot a vacant space with room for two towels and then a route through the colony to reach it. Sometimes you find a space that has just been vacated, gaping like the missing piece of a jigsaw and before you complete the puzzle again you notice the sand is already body-shaped with three hard mounds where nape, back and knees were and where heels, bums and heads have been, three slight hollows, still damp sometimes with blots like Rorschach tests but not quite so inspiring. You wonder if your own bumps will fit comfortably or not or whether you will have to do your own landscaping.

Once you've bagged a place you can look around and see if there's anyone you know and then you can wave or duck, depending. More usually it'll be someone B. met the night before. Not being Greek but Spanish, he knows how to have fun. He practises nightly, nevertheless, just in case he forgets, the danger of which I am a constant reminder. I interrogate him over break-fast or, if he wakes me, at four or five in the morning. If any of these characters are on the beach next day, as they usually are, I can see how good I've been at picturing. "You never said they were old" or "Samoan" or "transexual" or "very handsome" or "had such long hair." "Do you think he's handsome?"

Ten minutes after we arrive I see someone walking down the beach towards us. He's an air steward B. met the first night we arrived with his friend who works in the City. They were on the same flight as us from Gatwick. B. says he noticed them in the waiting lounge because one of them had stuffed a huge bag of Ecstasy tablets very obviously, like frogspawn, in his underpants. Since drugs are illegal I better not give them their names, although that unnecessarily criminalizes them. The one coming towards us now will be Muppet because of the way he opens his mouth and leaves it open. His friend who is nowhere to be seen will have to be Tuppet because he is interested in just one thing and, by all accounts, very successful at getting it.

Muppet, at any rate, is coming in our direction, but laughing so much at what he is going to tell us that he has to keep stopping to recover his balance. A group of Dutch men in front of us look at him as if he were a lunatic. By the time he is sitting on our towels he needs a minute or two to get his breath back, still bursting with laughter, anticipating ours.

He was fast asleep but was woken at three in the morning. Tuppet was shaking him frantically. They had to go out to the washing line and remove their towels. He was ordered to go and fetch their mopeds off the road and find somewhere to hide them round the back. He fixes me now, with a suddenly serious, wide-eyed expression – "Come on! Come on! You don't understand! It's very important! Hurry!" – before laughing again uncontainably and eventually resuming the narrative he was able to piece together.

His friend from the City had fallen in with some Italians. There may or may not have been an orgy of some kind but some kind of drugs were involved which gave him paranoid delusions. He had discovered a terrible secret of theirs. The Italians were mafiosi. Their bags were full of drugs and guns and now they knew he knew they were determined to get rid of him. The only chance of survival was to remove all traces of where they were staying, the motorbikes on the road above, their distinctive towels from the balcony. He was sure he hadn't told them what apartments they were renting.

Just as the story tails off, Tuppet himself appears, walking along the shoreline slowly, shielding his eyes. He could see from our faces we had heard about his fit of madness, but just as he was sitting down, he noticed the Italians. They waved, the three of them, from the back of the beach, nice boys, close to their mothers. Tuppet waved back and smiled without enthusiasm. Muppet rolled about laughing all over again, while his friend rolled his eyes up to heaven. "Did you see the parade at the harbour, in the end?" he asks changing the subject. "It was a bit disappointing," I say. "It was a model on horseback and six boys from the beach ..." but B. interrupts me.

The Persians came to Mykonos on at least one occasion, as Herodotus records, in 490 BCE. They put in here after the Athenians had defeated them at Marathon. It's impossible to recreate their mood but we can at least make a guess at it. It had not been a massive expedition for the Persians, that would come ten years later and end up even more badly, but it's quite likely the defeat had, nevertheless, astonished them. Mykonos might have been the first stop they made after leaving Attica. Datis, their general, managed at any rate to sleep a little for the first

time, perhaps, in ages, putting aside thoughts of
what had gone wrong and what would happen to
him when the Great King found out, or rather,
perhaps exhausted by them. What he dreamt,
says Herodotus, no one knows, but next day it
had consequences. At dawn he ordered a search
of every ship in the navy. A stolen statue was
found in one of them, predictably a tricky
Phoenician's. It was of Apollo, not from Delos
itself but from a temple to Apollo-of-Delos in
the territory of Thebes. Datis seized the evidence and asked the Delians to return it, but it
took them twenty years to comply. The sacrilege
was not quite a full explanation for the disaster –
a god's pleasure and displeasure must share the
same economy, and the statue was not gold, but
gilded – but it was at least a good opening gambit, considering the connection between Ahura-
Mazda and Apollo and the logic of all that
incense, which now looks like an insurance pol-
icy, a scriptwriter's sense of a plot.

Paradise is a Persian word, meaning a park or a
garden, but it's unlikely the Persians would have
found anywhere on this island worthy of the

word even if they'd landed. Greece is rarely verdant and probably never has been. Arcadia was always more imagined than real. Greeks knew this and looked enviously at the lusher landscapes of Italy and Turkey and wondered why on earth the Persians who possessed so many green paradises would be interested in their desultory patch. On the other hand, it also explained why the Persians failed. Paradise corrupts. And super paradises corrupt superbly.

Just as the desolation of Delos made the island offer itself as an empty stage for Apollo's birth and the throngs that came to commemorate it, so Mykonos's desolation brings people here today. All that clarity of beaches and seas is simply a sign of barrenness. Its seas are like swimming pools because they are uncontaminated by the dirty life of river silts and sea weeds, just dead sand, water and light passing between them unhindered. I saw an old sign pointing beachwards to a place called Plynteria which in modern Greek means "washing-machines" and imagine that for years washing clothes was all these paradise beaches were good for. Plynteria was also the name of a festival where they washed Athena's clothes, woven with scenes of gigantomachy, and took the goddess herself paddling in the sea, to get rid of all the dirt that had accumulated from fat-smoky lamps burning religiously throughout the year. During this festival secret rites were performed, all the temples were closed, and nobody did anything, for fear of disaster. It was one of the gloomiest days of the whole year and it was on this day in history that Alcibiades finally returned to Athens after years in exile abroad, sailing into the harbour with all the ships he had captured, music, musicians and poetry. Unfortunately on this day Athena's head was always covered. She could neither see nor hear a thing.

In 1628 Mykonos was visited by Charles Robson: "a barren iland of small extent some fifteene miles in compasse, wholly inhabited by poore Greeks, having but one, I cannot tell whether to call it, village or town of the same name with the iland, subject to the dominion and spoil of the Turks ... the barrennesse of the ile is much helped with the industry of the people, forcing corne out of rocky mountaines, scarce passable for men: yet they continue so poore by reason of the Turkes pillages, that unlesse they were merry Greekes indeed, any would wonder what delight they could take in living ..." This is why Mykonos is so pinturesque. A poor community without the resources for big houses in Venetian, Turkish or French style. The whole population budging up against one another in one remarkably sizeable town, the streets labyrinthine to protect the population from casual marauders. Low minimal buildings, humble Mykonos, ducking out of history or just ducking, a haven for British spies during the Napoleonic and First World Wars. "In all my life I never saw a place better peopled with woemen," Robson says spookily, "the number exceeding the number of men five for one: the barrennesse of the ile ..."

Melville also mentions Mykonos in his journals, but he doesn't seem to have landed there, which may or may not be significant.

Most of what Mykonos meant to the ancient world comes from its desolation. It was a tombstone keeping a heavy lid on all those odds and sods of Giants that Hercules swept under it. This myth gave rise to a saying which is Mykonos's chief claim to fame in antiquity, a saying useful in disarming a careless taxonomist: *mia Mykonos*, "all under one Mykonos." I imagine it as one of that elite group of sayings which carry such a weight of world-won wisdom and unexceptionable truth that the briefest incantation stops argument dead in its tracks: "It's a wise child ...," "It's an ill wind ...," "It's all under one Mykonos." I imagine sitting in on one of the dialogues Plato imagined and stumping his Socrates with my critique: "What you say is perfectly true, dear friend, but aren't you putting "all under one Mykonos"?" The others are silenced by my uncontainable wisdom, end of debate, much nodding then sighing and looking at watches, much wondering suddenly what to do next.

The saying implies that the Giants aren't quite extinct. They seem unhappy being lumped together and struggle against it. Only Mykonos keeps them in place. I note that children were sometimes buried in cities that dead adults were cleared out of. It's not that in times of high mortality children's deaths were brushed off lightly – another one bites the dust. It's quite certain there was much more bereavement, but no evidence parents ever got used to it. Rather, not having lived so much, children didn't carry so much lost life-force spilling over to haunt the living. And if dead adults had more residual power than dead children, how much more must dead Giants have had.

In antiquity, moreover, the spirits of those who died suddenly or violently were believed to have a special power, like the sour strength of unripened fruit. It is as if for the Greeks people gradually became alive, until they reached a peak full of power and danger. Only in their thirties and forties and fifties was this life properly cooked or dissipated so they would go more sweetly or softly into Hades' halls, without provoking a gagging reflex. Perhaps this is why hemlock was used in executions. It doesn't kill people before their time, it accelerates the process of dying and brings their time forward.

Elsewhere "One Mykonos" has a rather more positive force, announcing a regime oblivious of differentials. It appears in one of Lucian's dialogues of the dead. Pollux is about to be resurrected so Diogenes the cynic entrusts him with a message. Tell all the handsome men with their sturdy bodies that it's "all under one Mykonos" down here. There are no blonds here, no blue eyes or black eyes or rosy cheeks, no tight sinews or big shoulders, just naked skulls, barren of beauty. It reminds me of a line from the *Carmina Burana,* on the subject of Fortune: "Now indeed you may bear a luxuriant mane with even your forehead richly carpeted, but in time, as a rule, baldness of one kind or another follows, an *occasio calvata.*" Ancient Mykonians were said to have heads as barren of vegetation as the island they lived on. The slave in Terence's comedy should have known all along that he would never find a curly-headed Mykonian on the Acropolis. Such a creature was impossible. European visitors in the eighteenth and nineteenth centuries examined the islanders closely to see if it was true, taking advantage of their superior height. Some thought they could spot a tendency. Others absolutely disagreed. The other characteristic the islanders were famous for was a mean spirit and an exploitative approach to the rules of hospitality. "A neighbour from Mykonos" is one who borrows countless cups of sugar, but won't lend you a spade. This again seems to be a quality of the island itself, offering so little in the way of good life, yet unwilling even to allow Leto a bed for the night in marked contrast to her poorer neighbour.

Then there is the story of Ajax of Locris who found himself, finally, after ten years of imagining it, in Athena's temple on the Trojan citadel, the virginal centrepoint of enemy territory. Cassandra clung to the goddess's statue, but Ajax pulled her away violently, toppling the statue which landed on its back alongside the poor girl, staring heavenwards, while Ajax raped her. It was for this that a storm scattered the victorious Greeks as they left Troy thinking of home. Athena smashed Ajax's ship herself with a thunderbolt but somehow he managed to swim to a rock and thought he'd gotten away with it which was fine, until he said so, at which point the rock was split by a trident and he drowned. The Locrians had to send two virgins to Athena's temple in Troy every year for a thousand years to expiate the crime. Something they continued to do in the classical period. The girls had to arrive at Troy without being seen by the inhabitants or else be killed, apparently. I don't believe in such continuities, but I do wonder what it must have felt like when the tradition was first "revived." Ajax, meanwhile was buried on Mykonos after clean Delos turned him down.

I wonder if behind all these tales of buried heroes and Giants lies a little amateur archaeology. An earthquake in the reign of Tiberius caused great crevices to open up in the crust all over Italy and when men felt brave enough to go near them they found huge bodies inside. The tooth of one of them, more than a foot long, was sent to the emperor who ordered them to leave the rest where it was for fear of disturbing giant ghosts. He had a mathematician calculate the size of the head and reconstruct it. Thus satisfied he sent the tooth back for decent burial. Are Mykonos's Giants and hero, I wonder, long-forgotten elephants after all?

No similar concern for religion stopped

modern archaeologists tipping out the bones from a giant jar they found on Mykonos in the early Sixties and now the pride of the Mykonos museum. In the past few centuries cemeteries have been shifted to the outskirts again, but Christians do not seem to have lost their easy familiarity. The vase has an image on its neck in plastic relief of the Wooden Horse, the soldiers chuckling to themselves inside, visible through port holes the artist has made for us to see how smug they are, like a band of seducers wangling their way into their lovers' bedroom dressed as a present from Santa Claus. Below, scenes of women and children being assaulted and killed are shown, an extrapolation of what the horse contains. One of the women is elaborately dressed. One of them may be Helen or Cassandra.

The rest of ancient Mykonos consists of minor curiosities. A rich Mycenaean tomb was discovered in the early Nineties, but I don't know how rich exactly. In the second half of the fifth century Mykonos paid a contribution to the Delian League of one and a half, then one, talents. Not much, say modern guidebooks looking at how rich the island is today. Not so little, says the wise German *Encyclopädie,* considering how little the ancient island had to offer. It must have been making some money already from visitors to its fêted neighbour. Perhaps its economy declined a little when Athens moved the symbolic centre of the alliance to Athens in 454 BCE. Perhaps Athens felt a bit guilty and looked kindly on its request to cut contributions by a third. Its citizens were prominent among those who made dedications on Delos, as you might expect. There was an Anti(ochus); an Aristola; an Archippe and her husband Icarius; Demetria, Demoson and their father Eparchides; a woman called Simiche. Three slices of Mykonos were given by wealthy donors to the sacred island. One was the southwestern peninsula almost completely isolated by Ornos bay, another was adjacent to that. The third may well have been around Panormos in the north. Ancient Mykonos had two towns, the main one possibly where the modern town is, buried deep underneath; the other, bang in the middle of the island, probably near Ano Mera. They were politically combined in the Hellenistic period. They had a "democracy" or at least a town Council which made what decisions a little island might make. Their late coins carried images of Demeter, Poseidon and Dionysus. The sacred calendar lists a sacrifice to Seaweed Poseidon on the twelfth day of the lunar month that straddles New Year. The calendar stipulates a lamb with balls and that women are to be excluded. Finally there was a riddle that makes up the island's name from what a cow and then a trader says, that is "Mook" ("Moo!") and *"Onos"* ("sold"). (The Greek "u" (y) incidentally only becomes an i-sound in later Greek through a strange and energetic phenomenon known as ioticization. Moo like a cow and then gather your lips, while mooing, into a tighter sphincter remembered from French or German classes and if it eventually sounds like an "i" you have the island's name's history between your lips. I know it has happened often, but to find a filament of identity between what a cow says and what a mouse says seems to me a feat.)

Halfway through the afternoon the mood turns suddenly sleazy. A Dutchman is being lotioned by his puppy-like boyfriend, fifteen or twenty years younger, right in the middle of the integration zone. They are both nude. The man's penis starts rising and he moves to roll over but the boyfriend stops him and buries his face in his lap. A topless Greek woman keeps turning around to stare frowning, trying to be silently indignant, but because they don't notice apparently merely intrigued. The man takes his time to push the mouth away while people are saying "My god, look at that!" I feel as if I ought to disapprove and in another context I would, appealing to the dignified rather than the efficient branch of morals. But this is a seal-colony and I don't really bat an eye. The black of sex seems to emerge invisibly from the white of putting lotion on. An ambitious sophist or politician might say it was merely gradations of grey. But an ancient Greek who wasn't a sophist would certainly have thought it outrageous since they thought mouths were clean or ought to be and any kind of oral sex the most debasing act. A character called Demochares went in for this apparently and was described as "a courtesan with the upper parts (*ano meresi*) of his body." He scandalized the historian Timaeus of Taormina who said he wasn't fit to blow the sacred flame. In turn Timaeus scandalized the historian Polybius of Megalopolis by mentioning such dirt, sullying history with gossip and filth. It's hard to say if it was Timaeus or his critic who came up with the strange circumlocution for "mouth" and I wonder what a Persian's response would be, inasmuch as they seem to have thought the cleanest mouth so dirty it would have nothing to lose. Or was it rather that they thought flames were so clean?

Later a couple come back from the rocks with a little story to tell. They thought they had found a secluded spot near the promontory's tip. Then this guy with a snorkel had popped out of the sea and given them a shock and all the passion was lost. Ten minutes later they watch B. picking his way through the maze of towels. He flings his mask down and talks about what he has seen: some needlefish and an octopus. He had seen these two and wondered what they were doing there, but had missed the erotic implications altogether. He had thought they looked at him alarmingly, now I mention it.

At around five or six or six-thirty the beach empties. I am by now quite bored to death, again, but I concede that I am being cured of something. This cooking has sweetened, if only a little bit, my sour and bitter juices, and, despite the distractions, I've probably read at least a third of a novel in this one endless sitting, a book I would never read at home. We hang around. B. loves this mild warm time. He thinks it's what beach holidays are for. B. is from Madrid, more inland than any place in England, the centre of a high plateau, but he considers himself a citizen of the Mediterranean because he spent months, which he remembers vividly, each summer on the Costa del Sol in a big old house in the centre of Nerja with a huge avocado growing in its courtyard. The house is still there and the tree too, a monument to the luxury of space and long durations, rising above the boxed-in times of tourism that come and go around it.

Ficino, the Florentine who rediscovered Plato for Western Europe and found much wisdom therein, thought that scholars and academics, who spend their lives squatting in dark libraries peering over texts lit by the feeble substitute of fat-smoky candles, were sun-less grubs who lived under the sign of Saturn, which filled them with melancholia – although its English translation, "black bile," brings out, I think, more nicely, the bitter edge of academic lugubriousness. He suggested we surround ourselves with solar forces as an antidote: gold, butter, sunflowers, yellow things and blond boys. This was a purely biochemical reaction. These objects breathed good humour. They amplified the power of Light like lenses or relay-stations and would help alleviate the dark weight of academe as straightforwardly as chalk relieves indigestion. The blond men had to be young, he thought, because the light of older blonds was more feeble and less effectual. B. is not blond by any stretch of the imagination. In fact he's as bald as Mykonos. Nevertheless I use him to save me, not from sadness or depression, but from resentful compromises and sarcastic inertia. If you think this makes me sound parasitic you should be aware that there are two sides to this contract. He leavens my Dark Satanic Manchesterismus and in return I grab him by what's left of his hair and give him Second Thoughts.

We have an appointment at nine to meet some friends from London, who've just arrived in Mykonos, for a drink. Nine, because that will give T. time to take the protease inhibitors which have managed miraculously, after seven or more years, to purify his blood from all traces of the disease. His life had seemed securely bottled up. Now suddenly he finds himself with a luxurious future stretching out around him, not obvious like an island in an ocean, but patent like a plain. You don't need me to remind you that AIDS is far from over, but it seems, nevertheless, to be receding. It never felt like a plague, more like a pressgang, who would quietly enrol people you knew and impose a secret discipline. And mostly they would look exactly the same, but sometimes they would be wounded in some clandestine operation and sometimes you would suddenly notice that you hadn't seen them for ages.

Later we make our way to a ramshackle restaurant close enough to the sea to get splashed in the unnatural wake of a cruiseship passing far out enough to slip silently by. The food is fresh and fabulous, which is quite an achievement on this island for food. My tip for eating here is see what you're getting and avoid what sounds like cuisine. Conversation turns to G. He got ill very quickly last winter right in the middle of all the talk of miraculous cocktails and died, while everyone was assuming it would be another long haul, just off the Tottenham Court Road. He had been a dancer in a group, on television on Saturday night and a model, briefly. He appeared once in the Eighties on the back of a bus. Lately he had wanted to write plays and submitted manuscripts to the BBC, one of which he said had been accepted, though his friends raised their eyes heavenwards when they passed on the information. He could be embarrassing in restaurants but B. was fond of him. He was openly gay and lived his own life and had his own flat. It made him very attractive to a Spaniard and when he was gone, says B., it was like a whole section of the Underground was closed. Familiar routes were suddenly shut off permanently and you had to find new ways of getting there that weren't the same. "He could be obnoxious. He treated you like a joke." "You didn't know me when I first came to London," says B. "I was very confused. You didn't see the best of him. And I think you're wrong. He respected me. He asked me for advice." Says T., who never says anything nasty about anybody: "You didn't know him, James. He was a bit of a star, admittedly. You had to take him with a pinch of salt." "Yes ..." says B. "Yes ... yes ..."

If G. was bad, T. is a paragon, a bucket of clear cold water without being cold. You could rationalize it by saying he doesn't have grandiose ideas about himself, that he simply dealt with what luck had dealt him from one day to the next, that he didn't panic or he kept his panic to himself, but eventually you have to give him credit for not flinching from a particularly vehement form of truth. "Pinch me," he says in a mildly Irish Catholic accent. "Feel that? That's the drugs I was taking. They eat into the most basic layers of your fat in a way that even anorexics don't experience. And that will never fill out again." "They were experimenting on you," I say. "That may be" he says, "why I'm still here."

Conversation turns to the Twelve Gods Party. It's an American thing, apparently. It lasts about ten days. It's a bit of a wheeze for tour operators in league with resorts to raise the spirits and extend the season when summer is clearly petering out, but it also raises money for AIDS charities. They have events, a few discos, a party at the waterpark and then a night-long festival with a pageant which ends at dawn. There was a rumour this would have taken place on Delos itself, which would have been nostalgic, but they would never have got permission.

After dinner B. wants to go out. *"Un poco de alegría,"* he says, which prompts me to repeat my line about how the Spaniards are obsessed with being lively because they are terrified of death, which is why he leaves cupboard doors open and never finishes books. "At least at your funeral no one will be able to say you haven't lived." "And your funeral," he says, "will be months overdue, because it will take that long for anyone to notice." He thinks life has to be husbanded by means of generosity and the worst thing is to be mean. Cutting out coupons is positively ghoulish, like some kind of curse. To him Socrates' attempted libation makes all the sense in the world.

We go to the square where the gay bars are. It fills up at about midnight with a representative from every part of the gay diaspora, but especially Milanese. They always dress for the evening, often in black, and wear gold chains and rings. They seem to know exactly which yacht belongs to which designer. The enormous blue one is Valentino's, apparently, and Thierry Mugler is also in town. And, thanks to a new genius designer, Gucci is the thing to wear once more. They seem so soft these Italians, not effeminate exactly, but not exactly Roman conquerors either.

Italians first arrived in the area in the second century before Christ. Rome gave Delos back to Athens, ending a century and a half of independence and evicting the Delians from the island once again. It became a great emporium, a free port at Rome's instigation designed to punish the economy of an ungrateful Rhodes, a centre for trade in the slaves that were available in huge numbers from wars fought by Romans and the piratical chaos that followed in their wake. Delos, said later writers, could handle ten thousand – in Greek *"myriad"* – slaves a day and they remembered a saying which was already hard to believe: "Dock at Delos and your cargo will find buyers before you've had time to unload." In 134 BCE the slaves in the marketplace revolted, but not for long.

The last thirty years down to the year 89 BCE were the richest the island had seen. Athens too was minting it through some kind of discreet levy and started producing numbers of new-style silver coins. In 88 BCE, however, the phalluses on Delos started twitching again and a new power was felt in the region, Mithradates VI Eupator of Pontus, "Dionysus" from the Black Sea. Many Greeks saw him as a liberator and even Athens which had been Rome's faithful dog for decades switched sides. One day Mithradates' general arrived on Delos and all the Romans and Italians were killed, twenty thousand of them, apparently. The Romans distinguished themselves from their Italian allies energetically. At this very moment they were fighting against them in what is called the Social War. But abroad they seemed more similar and the Greeks called all of them *"Opici"* an insulting term used without discrimination. Here in Delos, far from home, Romans and Italians found themselves all under one Mykonos and then Mithradates' general arrived. Immediately after the massacre the Social War ended in reconciliation and Romans and Italians became one. I wouldn't claim Delos was responsible for the invention of Italy, but she certainly lent a helping hand.

Athens, meanwhile, was being punished. The general Sulla massacred the population, smashed statues and robbed Athena of all the gold and silver gifts she had accumulated over the centuries, carting off works of art, chopping down the groves of Academe, turning trees into siege-machines. It was the city's greatest ever catastrophe and archeologists have discovered many traces of the deliberate damage the Romans inflicted alongside the haphazard accidents of time. Most fighting was in the cemetery outside the Dipylon gate. Just next to it, just inside the walls, the Pompeion where people got changed for processions was destroyed by the catapults that missed. A ship was found at the beginning of this century off the coast of Tunisia weighted down with loot. A warehouse in the Piraeus, burnt down at this time, was found to contain bronze statues the marauders had overlooked, two Artemises, an Apollo and an Athena with her left foot wrenched off, quickly snatched from Delos, probably, by departing Athenians but never getting beyond the port. And all over Attica and Delos people buried coins in pots which they could retrieve when things quietened down, but didn't. The Romans left remarkably little damage in the cemetery itself, however, and relented eventually out of respect for the Athenians' distinguished ancestors buried like treasure in the ground. "We will spare a few of the living," said Sulla pleased with his formulation, "for the sake of the many dead." The Athenians inaugurated a new festival in honour of their liberator and showered him with gratitude. Some of it, in context, was undoubtedly sincere.

Delos, however, had had its day. Those sales of

myriad slaves seemed incredible within a few decades which is why they were mentioned in guidebooks. And the island was made an example of history's vicissitudes. It became a place only in discourse, a *topos*, a commonplace, but the island itself was nowhere now, aDelos, "obscure" once more. This is a set-up, admittedly, a scriptwriter's sense of a plot, but nevertheless it seems quite convincing. It fits what actually happened very nicely, as far as we can tell.

Geneticists think it probable that the character of each European nation was more or less settled thousands of years ago, after the first coming of agriculture in the Neolithic "New" Stone Age, each nation, in fact, a pulse or a wave, ripples emanating from a centre. The invaders recorded in history books – the Germans, Celts, Italians, Lombards, Greeks, Slavs – made only a tiny impact on these deeply stratified genes. These Italians in this square on Mykonos are the spitting image, at most slightly blurred, of the ones who terrorized the entire Mediterranean once and left cities destroyed and dogs – famously, deliberately, terrifyingly – sliced in half. The greatest fear I have of them now is that they will look at what I'm wearing and sneer.

There are plenty of Dutch and Germans many of whom have moustaches and look like dying Gauls, the ones whose strangely sympathetic images decorated Pergamum's citadel once and whose copies decorate the Vatican museums. There are some modern Greeks from Athens huddling together in a corner of their own. One of them has long wavy hair and is called Pan. There is another who now works in Germany and seems much more ebullient. We meet someone who gets annoyed when I ask if he's Algerian after he's said he's from France. He says he has been coming here for years, though he seems too young to be seriously nostalgic. And a Danish friend of B.'s French ex-boyfriend, who works in Paris and lives in London because he refuses to fund Socialismus. He's always smiling and handsome and having a good time and if you find yourself in the same place as him, you can be reasonably sure you're more or less where you're supposed to be on that particular night. A lugubrious Slovenian software designer talks in perfect

Bronze Athena (4th century) found in a warehouse destroyed at the time of the Roman sack

English of cruising London's gay bars on the Internet and *Absolutely Fab.* He enacts his favourite scene at ever-increasing volume, the clouds of gloomy melancholia evaporating as he approaches the punchline, until everyone around us is staring. "It was the mouse!" he shouts, laughing uncontainably, "The mouse! The mouse!" and then he's suddenly lugubrious again.

The Slovenian is also nostalgic for some kind of lost island, although the island doesn't seem remotely lost to me. I saw a girl on the beach carrying a stone to weight down a huge piece of Indian cotton cloth. "This is my stone," she said to her girlfriend. "It's the stone I found here ten years ago and I've used it every year since." She looks out over the beach and imagines using her stone to pin down a bigger piece of cloth that would cover the whole beach, purify it of straight people and turn the clock back twenty years. But these nostalgics are clearly not trying to recapture something. They come back to make sure their memories are in no danger of being surpassed. I don't understand this attachment, but I have to acknowledge from what I am repeatedly told that for many gay people this poor barren island has great symbolic value and Delos is merely a foggy destination they once had thoughts of going to, but never have. Some of them get quite aggressive when I suggest they really should.

Mykonos is where a lot of people found themselves for the first time, although some of them had to come back more than once to make sure. One of my friends used to come here when he was supposed to be straight. He would wait until his straight friends had gone somewhere else, then make his way to the gay beach. He would wander off onto the rocks and wait for someone to follow him and then he would conspicuously do nothing at all, to prove something to himself.

His family are Protestants who moved to Ireland from Scotland three hundred years ago. They live in an ancient house in the country near the border with the Republic. They had felt at home until recently when nationalist graffiti appeared on the walls near their house. Then suddenly they felt conspicuous. The house has a huge old wooden table which would fetch a fortune if ever it was sold at auction, but the house was built around it and would have to be demolished in order to get it out. It reminds me of a glamorous woman of a certain age we visited once on Ibiza. She smoked and swore and played Canasta and hated all the Catalan nationalism and the street signs which sprouted up suddenly in the Ibizenco dialect. "I feel less and less at home here," she said. "This place is becoming strange to me. I don't know it anymore." The British have been trying for years to show respect by pronouncing the island's name correctly, but they shouldn't have bothered. They were pronouncing it in the language of Castile.

There is something about gay people and islands, although Fire Island, an island off an island, is the only one you could call unequivocably gay. In Manhattan I saw a graffito which suggested putting all the faggots on an island. There was an obvious subscription which someone couldn't resist: "They did, honey, you're on it." The father of one friend wanted to put all people with AIDS on an island. I think he suggested the Isle of Wight. What would happen to them there was left to the imagination. I doubt they would have been well looked after and it made his son hesitate for longer before coming out. When he did, as it happens, his father was splendid. He became an instant "liberal" in this particular region of attitudes. The lesson you might draw is that the most evil prejudices may be casually held, which I think is true, but you also wonder what would have happened if his son hadn't said anything, whether, if someone did start to put all the people with AIDS on an island, he would have tried to find out what was happening to them, and having found out, if he would have cared. Jehovah's Witnesses were also rounded up in Nazi Germany and suffered as much as us. I don't know any Jehovah's Witnesses and I wonder, if it was just Jehovah's Witnesses, how much fuss, exactly, I would have made.

It reminds me of those fairytales in which a witch spares a man and asks in return for the first thing he sees on coming home. He imagines it will be his dog and thinks he's got away with it, but it's always his son instead. And the witch arrives to collect the boy and the family is disconsolate. Or like Rawls's theory of justice, which turns justice into a rational bet. He says, as far as I remember, that justice is the rules you would make for your society on the day before evolution, before you have become anything (clever, weak, strong, white) in particular and without knowing what place in it you (or your children) will be assigned. In the fairytale the son thrives, incidentally, and in some versions ends up marrying a princess.

Before we go back to the apartment we try to find Mykonos's only gay nightclub, but it's by now about three in the morning and we get lost. An American is caught in the labyrinth staring at a hand-drawn map, wearing shorts Europeans wouldn't be seen dead in after seven-thirty. "The Americans have arrived," says B. "Are you lost?" "You speak English," he says, apparently relieved. "Where are you from?" He is from California and designs shop interiors. His apartment is close to ours, as it happens. "He is a Sherpa," says B., nodding in my direction. "He will get us out of here." And I march off like a dog with instructions. After ten minutes I can announce with confidence that I know where I am. The route home is marked by the powerful smell of a jasmine which hangs over the passageway. B. says it never smells like this away from the Mediterranean. He says plants in cold countries are mean and you have to bury your nose in them to find out what flower they are trying to be. On Mykonos, by contrast, the jasmine is shouting, even at this late hour. It can be heard for yards around. I look behind myself triumphantly but there is no one to be seen. After a minute or two B. rounds the corner, having been running. "Slow down," he says. "I think you've got the wrong end of the stick. I don't think he's that desperate to go back to his apartment, not immediately anyway." It dawns on me. "Oh! God! Really?" The American turns the corner now, smiling broadly. "You know where we are now? Your apartment's near here, right?" "We have to be up early," I say. "Oh yeah!" he says, "So do I."

Next day we decide to go somewhere quiet and relaxing without *chiringuitos* and music. Ayios Sostes on the other side of the island seems the best bet and we tell T. and the others to meet us there. The beach is quiet and peaceful. The bay is deep and long. The wind is up, however, and blows enough occasionally to blow sand in our faces and flip over our towels. The locals say it always lasts an odd number of days, a minimal piece of prophecy which simply means if it's been blowing for an even number you can predict the weather a day in advance. Before going back to the apartment, after a day of this inconvenience, we decide to drop in on Superparadise. At the top of the steep road we can see the giant navy blue yacht pulling at its anchor and moving sickeningly slowly around. The wind has been a feature of the late summer in the Cyclades for millennia. On one of the three temples of Apollo on Delos they had an image of Boreas, the North Wind, carrying off a nymph and at some point in the fourth century he blew so hard he toppled Nicias's bronze palm tree and the tree knocked the Naxians' ancient Apollo on to the ground, where it has stayed. All that blowing has taken its toll on Delos's monuments. The lions, like Apollo, look as if they have had their features rubbed off, halfway to becoming pebbles or Henry Moores.

At the cocktail bar, there is a tea dance. There

are photocopied posters everywhere advertising some kind of music or movement from San Francisco called the "Vibe" which sounds like an aspect of Apollo. The Americans have arrived in force. Their gym-built bodies and loud voices seem to take up much more space than a similar number of Europeans. I quickly put my shirt on.

One of them has persuaded the owners of the bar to play a track which tries to be rave-like or techno but is thin and banal. Over the rampant beat the singer keeps repeating "People come together," like a maenad on Prozac. Another is carrying a book called something like *Riddlers of the Dawn.* It has passages marked like my grandmother's *Science and Health with Key to the Scriptures.* There are parts of it he wants people to read and moves around proselytizing. Although the confidence of Americans seems so alien, their passion for executions, their love of guns, you have to acknowledge that ninety per cent of gay liberation is thanks to them also. America is a battlefield of competing identities. I am not at all sure I could take it. For people in the Middle East, moreover, and Africa and Paris, English speakers share a mysterious common core which governs philosophy and economics and rains down missiles without calculation on dreadful renegades in Mesopotamia when they step out of line. You wonder how easy it is to resist the gaze of others or if the continuity they discern when they look over us reflects an awkward truth.

There are no lights on the road as we wend our way back and the lights from the mopeds are dangerously dim. But there is a vault of stars as low as the roof of an underground train stretching out in all directions, and a bright unclouded moon. We stop to look out over the boulder-strewn valley, feeling very much like tiny figures in a nocturne, all colours faded out.

We're leaving tomorrow, thank goodness, after two long weeks. My achievements are getting brown without sunburn, completing seven novels about half of which were gripping, one excellent and some others pretty good and not getting knocked off my moped. Now we're on a late bus to Mykonos's Hard Rock Café where there is to be the climactic party. Tuppet is flirting with a sleazy Greek of about forty whom he couldn't possibly be interested in, while Muppet is telling him to watch himself and asking where we've been. The tickets cost a fortune, but I am feeling much more lively now after two weeks of mindlessness and had to interrupt B.'s attempts to persuade me. I am pleased to note that after going out every night but one since we arrived here, he is completely exhausted, which is another achievement as far as I'm concerned. I don't have great expectations about the pageant, but this time I've been told there will be a full complement of Olympians on display.

The Hard Rock Café has gingham tablecloths, a swimming pool and a flashy old American car. I imagine the hamburgers are quite good. It looks like the kind of company where executives talk about standards and branding, but it's in the middle of nowhere and, as you have probably gathered, away from the spectacular beaches and outside the astonishing town. Mykonos doesn't look like a place at all so much as a geological deposit. The music isn't bad and I think dancing in the open air when it's warm is a wonderful experience. We get separated immediately. Muppet says he's had enough of tablets and reaches into his pocket to pull out the far-travelled drug bag, a largish plastic sachet, as dusty as a cereal packet with one cornflake left in the bottom. He thrusts it in my direction and walks off in disgust. It falls on the floor and I wonder if I should pick it up again. Drugs can be dangerous undoubtedly – a single Ecstasy tablet, apparently, can kill you (and cannabis can lead to indolence) – but they can also be perfectly harmless, it seems. You might have the best time you've ever had in your entire life, or you might, just possibly, die. Absolute prohibitions are irresponsible as soon as they are no longer generally obeyed. They put people on an island without teaching them about winds and currents and how to swim, which is fine until people find their way to the beaches where people are paddling and swimming and sailing and seem to be having fun. Then they have to discover the hard way the difference between paddling and being all at sea.

An extraordinary-looking man beckons me over. He's an Israeli from London. We fall into conversation and I ask him where he is from.

"Look at me," he says. "I'm smoking and drinking like second nature and enjoying myself tremendously. And I just broke up with my boyfriend because he drank and wouldn't stop smoking. If he could see me now, he would kill me. But what can you do? It's this island. Being on holiday, it's impossible to follow rules." I think back to Delos again, which had a synagogue, close to where the Samaritans who didn't like Jews but discovered away on Delos a certain neighbourliness, had their association and honoured the holy mountain Garizim. The Jewish god is known by his epithet *Hypsistos*, "the highest." On Delos, Zeus who had bagged a rather more lofty site on Mt. Cynthus, disputed this claim and used the epithet himself. This is a god who has some kind of identity at least with the one Christians worship, but on Delos just another god alongside all the others. He didn't seem to mind.

It was the Romans who insisted Christians worship divinities they didn't believe in, especially emperors, out of loyalty or for the safety of the state, and it was this insistence that made the Christians so uncompromising, so that within a century or two of being tolerated they ceased to tolerate any other god at all. The unusual oppression of Christians and their unusual oppressiveness are too much of a coincidence to ignore. It is out of persecution that the Christian monopoly was forged. God God has now been a major force in European religion for longer than Apollo, as far as we can tell. Soon he'll be catching up on Dionysus, Poseidon, Zeus, Athena and Ares. He has certainly made a difference. I wonder if you could calculate it and decide if it was good. Goodness is certainly a part of being Christian, but then the Spartans were good and the Athenians were good and the politically correct think they are better also. Elites everywhere have relied heavily on their moral superiority to maintain their position of dominance and I wonder if Christians are essentially good or just attach themselves to goodness to keep themselves in power. "I'm not Jewish. I'm Israeli," says the extraordinary man. "My family's very religious, but I'm not religious at all."

Later I meet a poisonous creature from New Jersey who is great fun and suggests I go and have my photograph taken for the commemorative beefcake calendar which is happening behind the flashy motor car. "I'm not beefcake, unfortunately. Do you think I could keep my shirt on?" "Oh God!" he says. "Don't they have gyms in Europe? B – S – E." He has all the lowdown on all the Americans who have made the trip and tells me the personal history of four or five of them, all the delusions they have about themselves and how they behave with their boyfriends. When one of them approaches the photographer he calls out, "No ... No ... No ... No ... No!" at ever increasing volume, until the man hears something against the beat of the music and turns towards him and smiles. His favourite word is class, that is, boys who have it and boys who don't.

B. meanwhile has asked a famous prostitute from London for a light. Unusually he is very handsome and has an image of a handsome beauty tattooed distractingly on his chest. He seems very nice and doesn't seem to lack dignity. Finally, there is a kind of synthesizer fanfare and the roof of the bar is lit up. Muppet has found us again and wants to know when we plan on leaving. I insist on staying until dawn. Tuppet is nowhere to be seen.

At the heart of the festival on Delos were certain secret rites. In particular there was a "crane dance" to commemorate Theseus's salvation from the Minotaur and a tree-biting ceremony which sounds much more like Leto's state of mind than all that gentle rain-like sweat. And at a certain point mysterious presents, conveyed, it was said, all the way from the land "beyond the North Wind," from the Hyperboreans, a happy divine people whom Apollo loved to winter among, which must mean from Scandinavia or Siberia or Derbyshire, arrived. These gifts were passed among the Scythian tribes who lived in eastern Europe and then went west to the Adriatic. From there they came to Dodona in northern Greece and passed to the Aegean along the mainland's eastern flank. Originally this game of pass-the-parcel avoided Athens altogether, but at some point the Athenians interposed themselves and from then on it went through Attica also. Finally it arrived at Delos, welcomed with the reverence due to such a far-travelled gift.

Originally the Hyperboreans had sent girls to convey these presents but they liked Delos so much they stayed and were buried there. After that the Hyperboreans didn't want to lose any more of their people to sunnier climes, wrapped their gifts in wheat straw and handed them into oblivion over the border. God knows what the Delians discovered inside. Perhaps it was bones of Mastodons. More probably, knowing Mystery Religions, it was something unspeakably banal.

At this point a woman stands up on the dance floor and makes a speech. She talks about where the money is going and announces the gods one by one. As she reads out their names they are illuminated on the roof, models or actors in Grecian costumes, although Hera and Poseidon look like the committee's friends. Apollo is saved until last. It might or might not be the same guy we saw in the harbour on a horse a week ago, but he is certainly splendid and they all look larger than lifesize. The roof is quite invisible now and lasers play over the divinities. You might be forgiven for thinking they were suspended in mid-air. The woman tells us about Apollo and how he loved Hyacinthus, but liked girls as well. The guy from New Jersey starts making discreet gagging noises, but I imagine when the show plays in AIDS awareness nights in Athens where gay people are all bisexual, that's quite an important point to make. There follows a rendition on synthesizers of an ancient hymn to Apollo reconstituted from a score discovered at Delphi. Then the lights go out and Janet Jackson starts playing again.

I wonder if Apollo would have enjoyed this night festival. There were no sacrifices, but plenty of accidental libations, albeit of beer, and he would certainly have felt nostalgic about the music and the dancing and the life.

The wind is blowing here too but more mildly now, and refreshingly. When it blows through the bar and across the dance floor, cigarettes glow more brightly. I light one in a quiet place and let it burn without contaminating it with my breath, for the god the Persians found on Delos, a fire fanned by the clean-mouthed wind. It burns down like a cartoon stick of dynamite. I hold it to my ear. It gives off a little heat and it sounds like sand.

Dawn comes and is worth waiting for, the whole island lying open around us, six or seven of us still dancing, one of whom is me. Muppet and Tuppet and B. are lined up with arms folded against a wall and waiting to take a taxi home. I feel as if I've achieved one thing more. The first plane of the morning swoops down and I know I'll be leaving this very day.

On the plane I see large numbers of people I saw on the plane that brought us here, but haven't seen since, and I think of all those other bars that quite outnumbered the gay ones by something like ten to one and those other beaches we never visited, and wonder how many gay men it takes to change an island. It shouldn't be too difficult to come up with a correct answer, plus or minus a margin of error. You could persuade holidaymakers to fill out a questionnaire before they turn in each night – Would you say you have had a gay day? Very, Not very, Quite, Hardly at all – or with more investment equip them with panic-buttons to press whenever they felt the island was coming over all queer. Meanwhile you could hold a gay cruise ship in the harbour and release its passengers one by one, tabulating the results of each incursion. Alternatively you could have teams of homosexuals, walking around the resort and coming out of the closet, according to a precisely calibrated system, step-by-step. A slight mince or a cravat, an over-tight T-shirt, over-white jeans, an over-cropped hairstyle, a full moustache, a hyperbolic reaction to a display in a shop window, a discreet holding of hands, a T-shirt with slogans, a tiara, a full snog. The research could be subsidized by the Ministry for Tourism. I will anticipate their conclusions. Gay people, being gay, have a particular valency, with only a very loose relationship to numbers on the ground. I bet only ten or twelve brilliant homosexuals at a peak of conspicuity could make the reputation of a medium-sized town.

Most of these people who fill the gay bars on

Mykonos will be back in the closet back home, giving homosexuality a massively inflated value, whenever and wherever it appears. We must be at least as common as Germans. Maybe only Indians and Chinese are less rare, but thanks to a thousand little gestures of discretion we have a capacity to make a spectacle, statemented, temporary stars. There are millions and millions of us, but we still manage to stand out, amazingly, in a crowd. Stardom can be burdensome. "It would be nice if America was just another country," said my Californian friend Tomás, once, "do you know what I mean?" I didn't at the time, but now sometimes I understand perfectly.

B. has been having a hard time coming out to his parents. As soon as the idea was mooted his sister sat on a mountain and made a warlike noise. And now he's finally out in the open his mother has been trying desperately to get him back inside. She made an appointment with a psychiatrist which he didn't keep and said, "You can drink if you're thirsty, but you don't have to have the jug on the table all the time." The jug being me, whom they blame for everything, me and London and being abroad. When he was little she had pushed him and his sister in a pram around the streets of Madrid trawling for compliments and getting them, but now she describes herself as the most disgraced woman in all of Spain. As he was leaving, she sat in a room with the curtains closed rocking backwards and forwards saying, "You're killing me," a performer of herself, which doesn't mean she is being dishonest. It's comical to describe it, very Almodóvar, but B. was briefly quite distraught. All his Spanish friends say he shouldn't have bothered, because Spain is Spain is Spain, not that the Spanish are prejudiced – they don't discriminate in law – it's simply part of their culture, the way they were brought up and Francism. But it cannot be hard not to overreact to people who queue so patiently to get into clubs and say sorry if they tread on your toes while dancing and generally keep themselves to themselves, any more than it's hard for a scion of a sink estate not to fall into crime. We should be tough on homophobia before we start analysing its causes. Creating a decent society and cultural history are two quite different things. B. meanwhile has stamped his foot and made like Mimas, responsible for nothing but being himself, sick of wandering obscurely, a suddenly obvious rock.

I ask him, considering it's been so much trouble if he thinks he shouldn't have bothered. He says not to tell his parents would be like not telling them he was the President of the United States. Shall I put that in, I ask him. "Only if you think it's interesting," he says. "It's your book. But don't use my real name. It's too personal. And I wouldn't want people to think I don't finish their novels, which anyway isn't true."

His father has been better and worries that his son won't feel like coming home so often. He is from Santiago, which means Saint James, from a big old house in the much-photographed square, at the very western edge of Eurasia. Santiago is in Galicia and his father finds links between his culture and the culture of Ireland and Wales, all witches and magic and fairies and halting halfway up the stairs. The apartment in Madrid is full of scallop shells. In the Middle Ages Santiago was a place people went on pilgrimages, enormous numbers of them in endless droves. A book was written to guide them. It says things like beware of the toll-collectors in Ostoba. They stand in the road with two or three big sticks and will beat you and search you down to your underwear. The author, a twelfth-century Frenchman, hates the Navarrese above all whom he says are descendants of Nubians, Scots and Cornish people with tails, imported by Julius Caesar. Hence they are a bastard race and their name comes from *non verus*, which means "not true." The Navarrese eat with their hands from a common pot and expose their genitals when warming themselves. They call God Urcia and the Virgin Andrea Maria. They put padlocks behind their mules and mares, to monopolize their sexual favours and engage in oral sex with them and women, which is why "they are to be rebuked by all experienced people." The Galicians, on the other hand, are almost as civilized as the French, although they are irascible and litigious.

The climax of the pilgrimage was the altar in

the Basilica which covered the body of the saint. The body was complete and impossible to move, apparently. The bishop Theodomir who discovered it tried and failed, which is why, says the guide, other cities which claim to have pieces of the saint are lying and should be ashamed. In Santiago the pilgrims could buy scallop shells as souvenirs, to remind them.

Coming from Santiago, B.'s father is the only person I know who must have some idea of what it would have felt like to be from Delos. The religious atmosphere rubbed off on the family who would get up in the middle of the night to pray but some of the women from time to time would go to bed and never get up again, afflicted with some vague boredom or illness and the family would say they were *encamadas*, "bed-ridden," and no one would ask further questions. B.'s father calls the book the first tourist guide, but a pilgrimage is hardly a holiday. We don't travel now; we make trips, passing from one place to another, by means of the same airports and similar planes. The places we visit are all islands now, discrete destinations with no journeys to get there and nothing in between; sojourns, breaks, respites, limbos, stays of execution, islands in time.

The plane doesn't have much runway from which to get a lift, but thankfully its wings are working and, as it banks, an image of the whole Aegean zooming away from us appears. Little white waves evenly fleck the blue water, Poseidon's horses, and Mykonos and Delos and Rheneia can be seen standing out barren brown from barren blue and then all the other rather bigger islands very vaguely in a vortex around them.

The Greece that ancient writers describe sounds very much like this one, same climate, same sea level, same rainfall, except that they seem to be rather better acquainted than you would expect with snow. It does snow in modern Greece, even, occasionally, on the plains of the ancient city-states. My friend who really was beautiful brought me the front page of a Greek newspaper once in, I think, 1983, to show me Athens knee-deep in the stuff. But he had never seen anything like it in his life and pinned the picture on his wall, better to accommodate himself to Oxford's bitter climate.

The reason that snow is rarer now is because Greece is not as high. It's collapsing towards the south and west, gradually dissolving. This seems obvious when you look at a map or when you see ancient buildings submerging. It's unlikely it was the first time, when Delos shook after the visit of Datis and the Persians. Little tremors happen at regular intervals as Greece itself subsides. I am not going to get all whimsical and say the ancients must have realized, but it reminds us that we have to historicize even states of being. The Greeks don't seem to have taken it for granted in the same way that we do. They put much more effort into becoming something and not falling back into oblivion once they had become, raising monuments for posterity. This is the only Greek miracle we need to think about, the energy they expended on leaving their mark, carving themselves on stones to act as guardians of their gifts, forever reminding those who came after that they had brilliantly been there first. All the marble that litters the place proved terribly useful for this purpose. Marble is metamorphic rock transformed under crushing pressures.

Delos and Mykonos and Rheneia were probably one place once, until the places that joined them vanished. There are certainly islands that rise out of the sea, but lots of others that are only islands because other pieces are missing.

It seems to be raining more heavily still. We managed to get drenched between the taxi and the door. There's masses of post which doesn't look interesting and lingering sand in our clothes. I long to sleep, but, as if to enhance the pleasure, I allow myself to be distracted by what's on my desk, something I was looking at before I left, the encyclopedia's entry on Mykonos. I notice something I hadn't noticed before, perhaps because it was in Greek letters, a short lemma preceding the one on Mykonos island. It refers to a little mountain called Mykonos next to Etna, mentioned in all of ancient literature only once and also a Mykonos topos, which might be the same thing. It seems a much more convenient place to put the leftover Giants when the big volcanoes had taken the biggest ones. I have no idea,

but as I finally subside into sleep, like sugar on a
cappuccino, B. already snoring, sand somehow,
despite our best efforts, in the bed, the rain still
torrential-sounding against the glass, I feel the
ground shifting
                    beneath

                        me.

                                    Hercules
                    may well have crammed all the
            Earthborn Giants under One Mykonos,

    but
    there were
    at least Two Mykonoses to choose from

                                    and

    maybe
    another besides.

About the Author

James Davidson was born in Manchester in 1964 and is Anniversary Reader in Ancient History at Birkbeck College, University of London. He is a regular contributor to the *London Review of Books*. His first book, *Courtesans and Fishcakes*, was highly praised on both sides of the Atlantic. It was chosen as International Book of the Year by Erich Segal in the *Times Literary Supplement* and described as "this year's must-pack paperback" by the magazine *Wallpaper*. "There could be no better 'popular history' than this," said the *Los Angeles Times*.